Moth Wing Tea

Dennis Cruz

Punk ⁂ Hostage ⁂ Press

Moth Wing Tea
Dennis Cruz

© Dennis Cruz 2013

Punk Hostage Press
P.O. Box 1869
Hollywood CA
90078
punkhostagepress.com

Editor: A. Razor

Introduction: Ryan Elliot Wilson

Cover Artwork Design: GROCE

Cover Layout Design: Geoff Melville

Back Page Photo: Annette Cruz

Editor's Acknowledgements

One of the pivotal moments that inspired the creation of Punk Hostage Press was a reading held at the Beyond Baroque Literary Arts Center in Venice Beach on December 8, 2011 that featured Danny Baker, S.A. Griffin, Iris Berry, myself, Annette Cruz and the author of this collection, Dennis Cruz. The reading was put together with the help of Richard Modiano, Rafael & Melissa Alvarado, Billy Burgos and it was well attended with many supporters of the L.A. literary community present. The energy of this reading was palpable in the air and it was the kind of reading that can't really be planned, it just happens given the right moment and all the right ingredients.

When Iris and I began looking at who we would publish when we undertook the press, all of those present and reading that night were at the top of the list. Dennis' writing has always struck a chord with me since I first read it some years ago, and to now be in a position where I would work with him to present such a collection is truly something an editor and publisher looks forward the most when undertaking these projects that become books. With that said, we are eternally grateful for all the people who made that reading possible, who make Beyond Baroque possible and who have supported this effort to come to fruition as book that really reflects the depth and scope of Dennis Cruz as a poet and voice that rises up so clearly out of the chaos that is the Greater Los Angeles area.

We would also like to thank Luis J. & Trini Rodriguez and their Tia Chucha Cultural Center for the inspiration not only to Punk Hostage Press, but also to Dennis Cruz as writer.

This book could not have been whole without the feedback given by Joe Baiza, Rich Villar, Steve Abee, Luivette Resto and once again, S.A. Griffin. We also want to acknowledge the introduction from Ryan Elliot Wilson, which is the perfect gateway into this book.

The cover artwork by GROCE and the design by Geoff Melville is a beautiful container for these words. All the hard work from Punk Hostage Press supporters like Kimberly Kim, Sonny Giordano, Lee McGrevin, Michael Juliani and Carlye Archbique is always crucial as well.

Punk Hostage Press would very much like to thank Annette Cruz for her support and input on this book, and for also being a supporter of Punk Hostage Press and the literary community that we were all born into together.

A. Razor 2013

Introduction

Whether the first encounter with Dennis Cruz's poetry is an accidental or conscious act, you cannot walk away without at least asking the question: was this meant to be? This sense of fate, or that something cosmically significant is taking place stems from the very core of what separates his work from others. His phrases, which fall down the page alternately in imploring roars and ghostly whispers, confront pain in all its forms and sources, from multiple and simultaneous perspectives that make up the poet himself.

Moth Wing Tea again finds Cruz dealing with the most vicious of demons: grief, abuse, drugs, cruelty—and yes, love—but this new work represents an embrace of the poet as bludgeoned spiritual warrior, looking the reader straight in the eye to drink in defeats and bellow out the notion that victory itself is illusory. In its place resides something more profound, something that might answer that question: was this meant to be?

A quintessential Angelino poet and performer for three decades, Cruz deconstructs the mythical L.A. and offers us much more than just the blood under the rug. Cruz's Los Angeles becomes a crucible for courage, a place for sublime humor in the face of suffering, a place to sip the life and death of this Moth Wing Tea.

Ryan Elliot Wilson
April 2013

for Annette

Table of Contents

I.

Accident	19
Lord's Prayer	20
Life, taken	22
Destiny	24
Scoring	26
no choice	27
staged	30
Sensitive Type	33
Making Connections	34
Matinee	35
root	37
Touching Love	39
Retrospect	41
Turn On	42
schizophrenic uncle poem #4	44
a little short	47
come on	49
Leap	50
final act	52
sick	54
Victory	55
heavy prayers	56
our inherent violence	58
vow	59
tired faiths	61
where I find terror	63
Good hands	64
tired mythology	66
PHILOSOPHROUS	67
fear of nets	69

II.

Medicine	73
no way out	75
not enough	77
Privilege	79
Typewriter	84
One of Those	86
promises, promises	88
side effects	90
lost, in denial	92
conditioned response	93
made from scratch	95
Trinity	97
afterlife?	98
Somnambulo	100
a small move toward a simple faith	102
Wonder	104
dance	106
recurring	107
Good-bi Lili	109
Inclement Love	112
old friend	115
as good as any muse	116
hollowed out	118
Weakness	120
Closure	121
my terms	123
Little Graves	125
Re-Creation	127
Fine, just fine	129
bait and trap	132
four one four	133
American Hotel	135
Suggestion Box	138

strangers	140
meaning	142
Death Trip	144
Legacy	145

III.

please, don't misunderstand	149
only god	151
hard up	152
safety net	154
wishing won't make it so	156
pass	158
dark inside	160
wrong turn	162
climbing and falling	164
Eye to I	166
from the POND to the OCEAN	167
fair	168
dime	169
absence	171
big questions	173
chance	175
Sick Leave	177
Cinema Verite	178
for the poets	181
making me	183
Seize the...	185
restoration	187
Inheritance Annulled	189
adversary poem #8	192
the one, true god	194
today	195
revelation	196
hang 'em high	198

permanent	200
Interpret This	201
this way	203
legion of you	206
church of ME	208

IV.

Alternative	213
keys	215
self-made monster	218
sitting in a chair	220
thanks for stopping by	222
recently passed	224
metamorphosis	226
4th floor window university	227
the rest of me	229
Jury Duty	230
transcendence	232
untitled paranoia rant #73	233
breathing in	236
The Club	237
Trick	238
surrender	240
me beast	242
spreading disease	243
Spectrum	245
one too many	247
never closer	249
Research	251
another blackout	252
Hereditary	254
more than you	256
my eyes will stop	257
mass-of-man	259

Butcher Hail!	261
making peace	262
Carpe Diem	264
mission	266
Where I can be found	267

V.

untitled paranoia rant #81	271
Portals	272
Con-Verted	275
Beats?	277
ruin	278
Good Times	280
take the reins	282
hope	284
Hand Me Down	285
moth wing tea	288
meth-scape	289
Vision Quest: Manhattan beach:	291
desperate like that	294
left to be	296
counting	298
clear	299
Brazen Enough	301
Boredom	303
comforted	305
back into your hole	307
as bad as it is	309
shooting in los angeles	311
anniversary	312
adversary poem# 67	313
witnessed	314
looking forward	316
forever	317

"Come talk to me. Talk to me of your terrors"

Colombian Star, The Concrete River
Luis J. Rodriguez

I

Accident

I go to lift the bandages ....just a bit....needing to reveal something about her. But I find nothing....just an emptiness, a void. I think that maybe a sexual preoccupation is the reason why I am unable to see her. I wonder if I'm looking past enough of her, to get to the relevant part. I'm not, of course, and she senses this, shifting slightly beneath the crisp white sheets. I avoid her eyes. Too much there. I can feel her trying to pull me toward her. She needs something from me. I sit there quietly, looking for it. But all that comes is the accident. I wish and wish for more, but it's just too big. Not enough room for anything else. A kind of fear settles in like a soft white fog. I'm almost comforted by it, but. ..I'm not. I tell myself she will be fine. Most of her will be. No scar. No limp. No obvious difference. Yet, I sit there, overwhelmed. Making silent promises to myself. I will make it up to her. I will make up for this. Somehow. I can hear her wetting her tongue, preparing to speak. I am filled with dread. I should have said something to her by now. She should not be the first one to speak. My mind begins to race hoping to beat her to it. ...but nothing comes to mind. She lifts her head ....I don't even move to help her," how are you?" she asks. And I just melt away. How are you? She's asking me. And I know it's too late now. I've blown it. She will always remember this like this. "I'm ok ...."I tell her. and that's the end of it. and we're never the same.

Lord's Prayer

Dear lord,
if you can
I want you to
bend me over,
I need the fill of your love.
This purgatory has hollowed me.
What have you done with my prayers?
My faith: a wine, that spills and spills
forever into you.
and your drunken hand
that fails to touch me,
as you miss and miss the mark.
Where are you dear lord,
when the flames lick and lick
at my heels?
Where were you when the voices came?
Did you hear what they said to me?
Dear lord, what happened to my mother?
Is she burning? I think I can smell that.
Late at night, when the world sleeps,
I can hear her screaming.
Why is that lord?
Are you not watching over her?
Or are you the reason that she's screaming?
Lord I want to touch you,
I want you to touch me.
Bend me over lord,
Let me have it.
I want it.
Everything
you have,
I WANT IT.

Give it to me.
please, oh yes.. ..
that's it...
yes...that's it....
yes.
thank you
thank you
LORD.

Life, taken.

where there were doors
I made windows,
and where they were closed
I made them to open.
one by one the fears receded like
shadows pulled back by the sun
and I felt the warmth
of light through the dark,
absolute and unrelenting.
the sound...at first faint,
like a tired breathing
about to stop...then
more like walls crumbling,
or old dead leaves, crunching
underfoot. and how many times
I counted...
ceased to matter
as lies opened and blossomed
into flowers of facts..
you were so right about me.
I really did want you to cry,
but where there were stops
I made lights turn green,
and when made invisible
I insisted you be seen.
seen first, ahead of the others
seen first,
when you said
I was lying,
when you said
I was hiding
something..

you were right
about me.
the sound at first
like it was dying out,
then more
just rustling
or hissing.
and then the one
clear voice..
faint but certain.
and I stood this ground
despite what it said,
and you were so easy
to open
after that,
and it's the same
for everyone now...
all so easy
to take,
and to open.
I wanted
to thank you,
for being my first,
for letting me take
more of you
than pictures...
I wanted to thank you,
for fighting
so valiantly
to the end,
for falling
as gracefully
as you did.

Destiny

I never think
to use those
paper
toilet seat
covers,
whenever I use
a public toilet.
it's a terrible
oversight,
I know,
it's just that
since
I don't
use them
at home,
all that
crinkly paper
just feels like
it's not really
me..
sitting there.
I like to feel
like it's me...
sitting there.
I tell myself:
everyone else
must use them
therefore,
the seat
is probably very clean.
I know:
but what if they don't?

well,
if that's the case
then maybe
I was
always meant
to go
ass to ass
with
all of them.

Scoring

cruising the shadows
ducking under trees
state park whistles and
sweaty eyes glistening
in the moonlight. ....
decades of warnings
coming to fruition,
fumbling
hungry with
a desperate lust
for oblivion.

no choice

I dragged her
across
the street.
she kicked
and screamed,
"be quiet,"
I told her,
but she
was oblivious.
I became impatient.
I knew
it had been
a bad
idea
but I needed
to be closer
to her.
I asked her
to come with me
but she refused,
and really
left me
no choice.
my car
was parked
in the alley
behind the Rite Aid
"SOMEONE PLEASE!!!
HELP ME FOR THE LOVE
OF GOD, HE'S CRAZY!!!"
her screaming
sounded

affectionate,
I knew
she would
warm up to me
eventually,
"SHUT THAT BITCH UP!!"
a homeless person
yelled
from behind
a nearby dumpster,
"okay."
I replied
and prayed
silently
that she would.
I had planned on
duct taping her mouth,
but Rite Aid
was out.
all they had
was electrical,
I couldn't work
with that stuff,
you could never
rip off
a clean strip
with your teeth.
I struggled
to squeeze her
into the trunk.
she was kicking
and screaming
like I was trying to
kill her.

she was being dramatic.
but that's
what I loved about her.
I can't wait to show her
what she's going to love
about *me*.

staged

there were
plastic
tubes
protruding
from her mouth.
her face and hands
had swollen
beyond all
recognition.
her head was dripping
with dark charcoal
fluid,
which I later learned
is often used
to treat overdoses
in an attempt
to absorb
the toxins.
her skin
seemed
at the point
of breaking.
her eyes were open,
an expression
of blind terror
hung on her face,
inappropriate
as the odor.
I searched
everywhere
for any remaining
semblance

of my mother.
the chrome
on the medical
equipment
seemed
unnaturally
polished.
the paint
on the walls
seemed
excruciatingly
bright
and fresh.
I told myself
I would not look
into her cold
dead eyes
a second time.
I told myself
I would not
touch her.
I wondered how
I had come
to be alone
with her
in this way,
at such
a time.
everything seemed
a bit staged,
and like
a bad movie
I reached
for her hand,

cold
and heavy,
and leaned in
to kiss her goodbye,
inhaling
the chemical
stink
of death,
fresh as
the flowers
they would lay
upon her.
I couldn't
help but notice
her manicured nails,
perfectly painted.
it seemed impossible:
one nail had
a tiny butterfly
painted on it.
and I wish
I could say
that I don't have a problem
with butterflies now
or that chrome
doesn't frighten me,
but I can't.
I wish I could say
I never did take
that second look
into her
cold dead eyes
but I can't.
I just can't.

Sensitive Type

at least Toby
had some balls.
he didn't pussy out
when I asked him to
handcuff me.
don't you know
some women
like to get slapped
and
fucked,
at the same time?
don't you know that?
not every girl
wants to be
'made love to',
some of us
just want to get
fucked!
don't you know that?
don't you know
anything
about fucking?
maybe I should
call Toby...
maybe he could
come over here,
and teach you...

Making Connections

the best way
is to befriend
a pharmacist,
who can
point you
toward
the proper
physicians.
the physicians
can recommend
reputable
psychiatrists
who can really
get down
to the
core issues
that are
causing
your
pain,
and prescribe
the
appropriate
medications.

Matinee

It was rumored
that one
of my uncles
might be
a fag.
some thought
he might be fucking
his friend Raymond.
Raymond
did
have a funny walk,
and his moustache
was rather thin.
this talk
was not allowed
in our house
so we whispered
about it
in the backyard.
I was worried,
because that uncle
was my favorite,
the only one to ever
take me
to the movies.
I didn't know
what I would do
if he turned out
to be a fag,
but I was sure
it would put a stop
to any more movies,

and that was way
more important
than whether or not
he was
fucking
his friend
Raymond.

root

the bed is broken.
it makes an awful
sound,
when I roll over
in my sleep.
the sound
wakes me up,
and I sometimes
become angry.
there is something
wrong with
the plumbing.
terrible smells
come up through
the sinks
and through the floor.
a kind of sewage,
I suspect.
sometimes,
this makes me angry.
if the litter box
is not pristine,
the cat defecates under
the bed.
this sometimes occurs
in the middle
of the night.
if I am asleep
it can take
a few moments
to determine
if the odor

is sewage
or feces.
often...
this angers me.
this alone
does not,
in my opinion,
constitute
an anger problem.
but the
other things
do.

Touching Love

she died alone,
I wonder how I'll die?
I hope it's fast.
faster than her.
I wonder how you'll die,
how my son will die.
I wonder because
I can't stop myself.
that's why I can't
mutter what I'm thinking
out loud.
that's why I get scared
when you catch me
muttering to myself.
I know we're going,
I just don't know
where,
or when.
not sure
if I could handle
knowing
anyway.
not sure if
I want to know
much more of
anything
anymore;
except
more ways
to make you
laugh.
because I miss that

more than anything
when I don't have it.
I miss that more
and more
as I get older.
lucky thing to find
all this
thinking
has led me here.
right where I started,
when finding
purpose
seemed as easy
as touching
love
with the palms
of my
stupid hands.

Retrospect

So I say to him,
man...I used to get
so many burns
on my lips
from smoking crack
cause I could never
wait for the
fucking pipe to
cool,
and he was like:
that's why you
got to use at least
three pipes.
shit.
now I feel like
I've got to
start up again,
like I was
doing it wrong
all that time.
I know it sounds funny,
but that's the
kind of thing
that'll keep me up
at night.
that's the kind
of thing
that could really
you know....

Turn On

turn off the
television.
try to look
at something else.
get up from
where I sit
to watch television.
make a new area
to sit,
somewhere that
faces
away.
close my eyes,
remember the
patterns
the acid
used to make.
get nostalgic
about the acid,
the acid music,
the acid friends.
consider calling
the coke connect.
decide against it.
bask in the night's
first
small victory.
stop and rest.
gather
my
strength.

hunch over
and do
three
powerful
push-ups.
feeling stronger
now.
dust off
the typewriter,
slip
in a sheet,
and turn
it
on.

schizophrenic uncle poem #4

we were lying
there
in the dark,
me on my bed
him on his.
it was very late
almost early.
I was trying
not to listen to him,
but he kept
giggling
and scratching
at himself.
I had the feeling
that there might have been
someone else
in the room
with us,
but it was
just a feeling.
his laughter
was perverse,
I hoped
he wasn't
masturbating
or touching himself
anywhere
inappropriate.
he had been known
to blur that line often
and I was a bit
afraid.

he began
calling my name
"Dennis, Dennis! Hey Man!!!"
I didn't want to know
what he wanted
but I didn't want him
to get up either.
"What?"
he asked me if
I would shave the
hair off his balls.
I thought he
was kidding
but I could still
hear him
scratching,
then he asked
if I could help
with the hair
on his back.
the itch was driving
him crazy, he said.
I thought
it was more than
the itch
that was driving him.
his scratching
grew
in intensity
as did
my fear.
I worried
that he might
actually

draw blood.
for a moment
I considered
shaving him,
but could not
come to grips
with the idea,
then
just as suddenly
as it began,
it stopped.
the cackling
the scratching
the speaking
and we
both drifted off
to sleep.

a little short

she'd been snorting coke
all night long
licking the last bit
off the motel counter
at about five thirty
in the morning.
check out
was at eleven.
she spent twenty minutes
snorkeling up
the chunks
lodged in her throat.
it was disgusting.
he thought about
fucking her,
then spent thirty two
minutes
struggling through
the porn pay-per-view
prompts on the
telephone ordering
service.
finally he managed
to get people
fucking on the television.
the fucking people
were synthetic
and depraved.
he moved in
to kiss her.
she tried to ignore
the foul

of his breath,
as he flicked
his tongue
in and out
of her mouth.
she hoped the
chunks from
her throat
would dissolve
in her stomach
to distract
her away from the
coming sun.
she told herself
it was time
for a change
but wanted
to go out
with a bang
she told herself
she loved him still
she told herself
lots of things
she could never
remember
in the morning.
and finally
they did fuck
and it was
fast and unmemorable
and more than
a little short
of a bang.

come on

and with my veins
pushing up
against my skin
something like wind
is heard,
a wave of moth's wings
inverting
and ripping free
and suddenly
this cavity
finding its fill,
a backward
brimming
of chaos flutter
and my eyes
roll back
into the warm
wet
dark.

Leap (for Tsen)

This place:
a dark forest
of splendor
and fear,
destinies
lurking like
dozens of eyes,
peering at us
from the depths of
this unfathomable
dark. And we listen
to the whispers
that sway us to
and fro,
searching for the
faintest hints
of hope,
then suddenly,
if our diligence
permits, we
catch the faintest
glimmer,
the slightest
twinkle
that beckons
from just beyond
the deepest
shadow.
It is at this moment
that all our learning,
and all our faith
asks of us

one small leap.
this invitation,
the beginning
of our reward.
and should we
possess the courage
to take
just one step
toward it,
the path
shall open
and all
will be
revealed:
all that is
good,
and true,
and pure.

final act

She didn't slash her wrists
you didn't have to see that,
you didn't have to clean that.
you should consider yourself lucky
it could have been worse,
she could have left a note.
think about that, trying to decipher
all the hidden meanings,
the symbolism,
what may or may not have been
personal references to you.
she could have taken your brother
with her
but she left alone.
that's commendable
takes courage,
conviction.
one final act.
one last stance
against whatever,
she thought to be unjust.
she could have lived
and sucked the life
from all that loved her.
she could have turned
INTO
something wrong,
something worse
than what she was.
she didn't stuff
a gun into her mouth
and pull the trigger,

imagine?
someone would have
had to clean that up.
someone would have
been,
the first one to see it.
she didn't leave
that kind of a mess
just this stillness,
this tidiness.
and there is
nothing
left of her
to blame.
just as she wanted it:
something ordinary
something tragic
something human.
she didn't slash her wrists,
she didn't burden anybody
with that.
finally, something
worth
remembering.

sick

the dead cat of
your face,
pressed against
the window.
begging and crying
and you know
how much I
hate it when you cry.
the way your mouth
turns down.
the pathetic quiver
of your pleading
voice.
the dirty frying pans
of your eyes,
boring into me
like a fire
into the dry
leaves of me.
and I just
want to be left
alone with my
sickness...
so I can die
the slow death
of living.
so I can
keep you safe.

Victory

one ordinary
day after
the next.
brush teeth,
ignore pain
feign desire.
off to work
back to home.
search for
something
to hold
my attention.
put another
evening
away.
make another
day die.
try and remember
the things
that make it all
worthwhile.
peace, love,
family.
recreation?
but the light
dims.
and with it
so does the hope
and I wonder why.
is it boredom?
whatever it is,
it's winning.

heavy prayers

wet with the
sick-fuck
mind-spill
all turned over,
burning evenly,
slowly.
this rage
like angels
caught in razor wire,
this head
just shot gunned
into no composure.
so much death
on the corner,
so much fever
in the drying
puddles of blood.
dead mothers
and scared
reluctant fathers.
lost children
drowning in
oceans of knowing
welcoming sleep
like infants
swimming thoughtlessly
back to the
whispering warmth
of the womb.
wet with this
river of weeping
crippled by this

light-fed illusion
and the dreams
come
like plagues
in the night
relentless
in their terror,
unforgivable
in their pertinence.
and all this dread
just draping over
bloodshot windows
to the soul.
hope broke as faith.
knees too worn
to support these
heavy prayers,
and the lord
finally
just too distant
to care.

our inherent violence

beneath the knuckle,
the curve of bone
says more of it
than any words
could tell.
beneath the skin,
the blood
driving.
the rhythm
speaks better
of it,
than all our
tired music,
than all our
dreadful songs.
it is no wonder
that only
a distant silence
prevails,
only
a quiet failing
rises to the
occasion.
leaving only
a tiny trail
of history
in its wake.
a tiny trail
of blood
and bones.

vow

every day I clean
and straighten
and assemble
and gather,...
and I
arrange
and make good
what chance
has baddened,
but the chaos
finds her way
and the work
leaves me tired,
and so off to
bed I go,
leaving
more for the morning.
and when I wake
the sounds of
my discovery
mask
the silence
of my refusal
to get to the nitty-gritty,
to the muck
of the goddamn thing.
so I resign myself
to falter,
lay dust devils
to cleansing alter,
and in defiance
light a candle

against
the up and coming
wind.
vowing never
to forget
that mother
made her bed
before
she put it all
to an end,
before
she found
a way
to bend.

tired faiths

the streets are lined
with ashtray dirt
as the whore peels scabs
from beneath her skirt

but nobody weeps
for the crack heads
or the bandits.
all eyes on the prize
as the libraries
shake the books,
back into their places
and the dead fish
rip the hooks,
out of their faces.

clocks ticking backward,
away from all the noise,
as our dreams die,
elegant and poised
for destruction.

oh but the voice we silence,
lying naked in our beds.
replaying impulse
after impulse,
like blood spilling
out, and back into our heads;
as the dogmas weave and blur
into one another,
one last gasp
before the demons

shed their cover,
and the light dims
just as it should.

dark now.
faiths burning,
as clergy scramble
for the warmth of sex,
begging god's mercy
to grant them a test,
and the night, like a whore,
delivers.
a paradox to ponder
as the black sky spills
its dark wet rain.
streets blanketed
and earth,
burning and turning
in her sleep,
starving for oblivion,
and the insects
sing their praises
to the machines.
.
all hail the butcher's cleaver
that we may one day see
the origin of our meat:
threads weaved into braids
braids knotted into nooses,
nooses we hang
our tired faiths
from.

where I find terror

In the eyes of the corpses
bitten by crows.
In the smiles of generals
sending flowers
sending flowers....
on the butcher's apron,
where the blood makes patterns
like beautiful constellations.
on the beads of sweat,
dripping from
a prostitute's brow.
beneath the janitor's nails.
in the meat
stuck between
the cannibal's teeth.
in the heart of love.
in the hands of children.
in the suffocating
arms
of god.

Good hands

all those pretty knives
shining,
and I can't decide
which one,
to touch you
with.
you've been
so brave these
last few
days,
I want to
reward you.
your eyes always
flicker
when we meet,
in my dreams.
and your voice
becomes
just
hissing
and crackling
and
the static
hides your feelings.
I don't like that.
I want your feelings,
out in the open,
where I can
see them.
I get confused
when you cry.
I think you're

hiding something,
something I want
revealed.
perhaps
the cleaver?
yes...
I think we'll
start,
with the cleaver.
don't cry...
I've done this
before,
you are in
good hands,
and I don't
like it
when you cry.
just be still.
very, very
still.
that's it
ok....
that's it
now...yes
now
you
can
cry.

tired mythology

we rely on:
old hallucinations,
dated conclusions,
monkey drivel
served in
bowls of progress.

the truth,
like our entrails,
flung into the
glittering stars,
a blood feast of
history and
divination.

the awkward fumbling
of our need;
birthing ritual.
blind to the notion
of self against
wall after wall of
THEM.
no new gods,
no new miracles,
just the same
old
tired myths,
urging us
to fight.

PHILOSOPHROUS

I sat down
hard,
feeling my belt
cutting into
a roll of flesh.
I cursed myself
silently
but made
no promises
to change.
I coughed,
hard,
trying to dislodge
a bit of phlegm
that never
seems to go away.
after spitting,
I lit a cigarette
and inhaled
with what I believed
to be
great abandon.
I took a long
hard
drink of beer
and ignored
a stabbing
urge to urinate
and pondered the likes
of SARTRE
and NIETZSCHE
and whether or not

I would ever get it.
I thought of a friend
who is really
trying to read
JAMES JOYCE.
I farted softly
thinking
that perhaps
I never would
read JAMES JOYCE,
perhaps
DOSTOEVSKY
and HESSE
would be enough.
and now
BUKOWSKI
is dead too,
no matter what
black sparrow
might have you
believe
so I sit,...
and drink,
and smoke
and wait for
WAGSTAFF
and ABEE
to bring me home
don't let me down
fuckers,
I'm counting
on you.

fear of nets

I was a puzzle
of worms
in a bad bed
of dreams,
gone sour.
and your hands
were like bodies
of their own,
with arms and legs
and eyes,
so that when you
touched me,
it was more like
wrestling me..
down.
and you were
such a net,
when I was just
a nervous,
writhing,
heap of snakes.
and you were
never afraid,
and I always was.
now,
looking back,
I'm glad I
braved you,
even though
you were never
anything
to fear.

II

Medicine

Too many odors/colors and I can't get my car clean and I want to stop at 7-11 to get something...maybe a packet of that ephedrine up stuff or a red bull even though all I really want is to have that glow of the overhead lights wash over me but I know if I stop in there I'll probably linger too long in the wrong isle, like where they keep the cough drops and antacid and then the guy at the counter will lay his eyes on me and I hate that because I can feel them but just driving around isn't cutting it and I don't want to start circling the park anymore cause I know I'm too chickenshit to score anything but I really got the cravings real bad and I can't hang in my own head for much longer like the thinking is just piling up like real dirty laundry or the trashcan spilling over onto the floor...I need medicine, I don't feel together... there's too many people out on the streets tonight.... I stay up late for the quiet but it's not quiet and I'm running out of choices. I knew tonight would end up like this, I knew as soon as I got up this morning....maybe I'll just hit fifth and main and get some codeines or something...maybe I can get valium. Valiums are getting hard to find though..... I know if I can just get past tonight I'll be okay the rest of the weekend a few more hours just a few more hours and this fuck of a mindset can find a place to rest no solutions just action to pull attention away from my inactivity and the odors seem to be ganging up on me and I can't get the smell off and the wind isn't helping and I'm circling the park again...looking for a pair of eyes to shine out from behind the

bushes, listening for whistles or whispers ....and now
I've parked the fucking car....
but I don't give a fuck because I really need some
medicine because I'm not feeling so good and the
night is young anyway so fuck it... just fuck it...

no way out

three hundred red
exit signs
lined up
in my head,
and this dementia
is no reason not to
look me in the eye.
it's these discomforts
that remember us
when
we've forgotten how
to feel.
from cesspool of pity
to lake of fire,
from revelations
to affirmations.
three hundred
red
exit signs
and us like
soft plants thinking
exits lead outside
and by us I mean we,
and by we, I mean
me, and by me I mean,
every one of *I* but them.
and the cold within
and the bored without,
and we don't take
our reasons
to the vet,
with all their rabies

with all
their teeth
gnashing,
and we just thinking:
follow the lights
toward the back
of my watch.
follow the lights
toward the lure
of the dark.
this plan,
nothing more
than a gentle
reverting.
nothing more
than a mirror
facing down.
another exit
lying,
leading to
another
no
way
out.

not enough

these cold dead fish
of my eyes,
like friends
too high
to recognize,
and you go on instinct
like following footprints
in the snow.

the meat locker clean
but for the blood,
and we the butchers,
the carnivores,
just smiles
and appetites.
as natural
as plague,
or famine,
or war.

these heart pipes
freezing down
in the deep beneath,
like our fingers
plunged into
the wet
of our lives.
this sunrise too bright
to love,
our nimble thoughts
burning
in the flames

of our beliefs,
fighting
for survival.

no words left,
no words right.
teeth marks
on the photographs,
black lines
down the middle
of the pages.
these cold dead fish
of my eyes
seeing nothing but
failure.
nothing but loss.
too much cure,
not enough disease.
not enough death.

Privilege

I am at the DMV.
waiting in line.
it is the line
you wait in
before you get
to the actual line
you must wait in.
I am wearing
leather shoes
with gigantic soles,
the punks call em
creepers.
seven years ago
they seemed like
the ultimate shoes,
but now
they are hurting my feet.
they are new, and
the line is long.
eternal.
my hangover takes on
new dimensions.
my stomach rumbles
and my rectum begins
to quiver.
I have been holding in
a terrible shit
for well over an hour.
it is a wet shit,
I can tell.
I am holding on.
my license has been suspended

for the past seven years
the shit can wait.
I am almost there,
7 years of cop-fear
almost over.
then it is done:
they take the thumb print,
shoot the picture,
and I rush to
the public toilet.
there is only one stall.
the lock is broken.
the door won't
stay closed.
the DMV is very crowded.
I sit down
hoping it will all
be over quickly
it is not,
of course.
it gives me trouble
right from the start.
all manner of cramping
and splashing.
I begin to sweat
and worry when
suddenly
someone walks in and.....
opens the door to the stall,
as I struggle
caught, suddenly,
in the bitter-sweet rapture
of mid-push.
I knew it was only

a matter of time.
the man seems to linger
watching me for
a few seconds longer than
what would
seem appropriate.
he apologizes finally
and leaves me alone
to finish my business.
I push on, trying to
coax my ass into
finishing.
finally it is over.
I reach for the roll
of paper,
only to find:
there is no roll.
instead is a dispenser
filled with hundreds of
little tiny individual sheets.
I pull them out
one by one
trying to gather enough
to build a formidable stack.
my ass has made
quite a mess of itself,
the tiny sheets
seem ridiculous,
they are no match
for this shit.
I take the first swipe
at my crack and
pull out the sheets
now covered with waste,

and begin to
fold them in half
preparing for the
second swipe,
when suddenly
someone else comes in.
I begin to pray:
*please don't open the
door to the stall*
someone opens the
door to the stall.
it's a large latino man
with thick brows.
he looks at me in the eye,
he looks at what's in my hand,
he looks at my shoes,
he looks at me
one more time
in the eye before
finally deciding to leave.
this one does not apologize.
he is upset that he
had to see a man
holding his own shit
in his hands.
I am upset that I
had to be seen,
holding my own shit
in my hands.
I finish wiping
and leave
without
washing my hands
it is a

beautiful day
outside
and I am once again
a licensed driver
and it is
an honor,
and a privilege.
I walk over
to the bus stop
feeling proud.
feeling.....
like a
new man.

Typewriter

I lean
the machine
closer,
more
into myself.
more into
the meat of me.
as if this,
would somehow
human the thing
into
communion,
but
the truth
of my material
is too much
for it
to carry,
much less
hold up.
So I carry
it
and myself
away,
like
a burst of fog
suddenly
burning off
beneath the
heat of the sun.
I know we will
have

our time
together,
but it cannot
be forced
and should not
be pushed.
genius can
never be
rushed.

One of Those

a day for
slamming
doors.
nailing them
shut.
eyes open
for no good reason.
keep the curtains drawn.
tear the phone
from the wall.
eat nothing,
but drink heavily.
today,
THIS DAY,
custom built
for seething.
harnessing rage
to do
the devil's work.
someone's got
to do it,
and this day
has called me
out.
no provocation,
no reason,
just a slow
burning
fire
of hate.
fuck forgiveness,
fuck remorse,

nothing to do
but wait.
let the anger
run its course.
this is
my place
of grace,
this is where
I shine.
I will be here
for as long
as it takes.
I've got nowhere
else to go.
I've got plenty
of time.
bring me
all your love,
and I will show you
how easily,
it can be destroyed.
bring it on,
I dare you.
I'll be waiting
right here.
I'll be waiting.

promises, promises

I have become
what I've always
feared.
putting my
free moments
to death
with talk of work
or politics.
even this poem:
a feeble attempt
toward a quiet
turn,
as death
hovers
smiling,
all too knowing.
the night,
a quiet challenge
to all my
inherent noise.
with me
always gone.
gone to sleeping,
gone to rest,
I have become
what I promise
to reverse,
just as soon
as I get
some time
to myself,
a day off

from work,
some much
needed
R and R,
a decent
vacation,
a drink
or two
beneath
my widening
belt...

side effects

I see advertisements
on the television,
for new
and exciting medications,
though
the ailments
are sometimes vague.
I find that curious.
the actors
in these ads
seem happy
and confident,
no doubt
grateful
to have overcome
such
heinous afflictions.
yet somehow
the message escapes me
and the curiosity
is starting to get
to me.... and now:
I am having trouble
sleeping,
I've been experiencing
dry mouth
and fatigue,
some sexual
side effects
a bit
of rectal bleeding
on occasion.

I seem more irritable
and slightly out of breath.
I've been having
increasing thoughts
of suicide
and there are these
facial tics that I worry
may become
permanent.
I am hoping
I can take something
for this.

lost, in denial

the paths
merge
at the apex
of knowing.
and
the fork is silent,
as it was
in the beginning.
my retrospect
nothing more
than
reflex,
offering
no indication
that a way
was lost
or a path
chosen.
and now only
this
shuffling
forward.
lacking direction
and surely
heading toward,
an inevitable
end.

conditioned response

tonight I
re-invent
this death,
reinvent
its meaning,
its relevance.
tonight I convert.

this night
is all mine
to squander,
this moment
only mine to stop.

something moves
through me as,
something else
surrenders to it.
I observe it all
from a quiet
distance..
like a puppet show
made up
of shadows.

and the light
too frail
to brave the dark,
finally recedes.
something delicate
in me
approaches,

and I soften
in preparation,
afraid
I might
harden it
with my
thinking,
but it knows me
too well
and passes me by
leaving a warmth
that fades
as quickly as it
came.
and I only
feign surprise,
knowing
my performance
isn't
fooling anyone
not even me.

made from scratch

all the cosmic
intersections
cross jettisoned into
one clear
but dangerous
path
on fire,...
and us,
of course,
too reckless
to resist
the pull
of so much
symbolic clash.
and so we
danced in flame
and fury
till all that was
left
was one
uncompromising
question
that neither of us
would dare pose.
now the answer
sleeps beside us,
gurgling
and farting
in his sleep..
blissfully unaware
of the battle
that

brought him
here.
ignorant
of the surrender
that caused him
and the fire
that continues
to keep
him
warm.

Trinity

When we're together
I become a woman
and you become
a man
and then
something else
happens:
A third thing
that is neither
you
nor me,
joins us.
some call this
God,
others Magik.
I call it
nothing.
to attempt
to name it
would be
to pretend
to understand.
But I will say this:
whatever it is,
It is because of
and/or
more
about
YOU,
than it is
of me.

afterlife?

The void:
like a clean room
in a dirty building.
I shuffle about
the infinite
gloom,
wiping away
the residue of
another bad dream.
I gather my things
and assemble them
in an orderly
manner.
In preparation.
I wonder
if I'm awake.
the vast unknown
beckons,
and I'm afraid
I must be going.
I write her a letter:
Please don't remember
the things
that left
a bad impression.
instead ...
try and recall
those fleeting
moments
of laughter
and joy.

I fold the letter
three times
and tuck it
beneath
the lamp
by the stereo,
marveling
at all
the empty
space.
then I walk,
slowly
but purposely,
away.

Somnambulo

I'm sleeping now:
walking and talking
but not awake.
dreams float a bit
behind my eyes,
can't remember them
anymore
but I know
they were bad;
relatives,
or demons,
or lots of
walking around in
tiny circles.
I wanted to say
that I loved you
this morning
but I got
the feeling
we were fighting.
we weren't though
were we?
now I've made it
worse...
It's so hard to believe
I've become
estranged
by default.
I want to
hold you
but ...
I get stuck...

who did what
to who
first..?
or why?
I just want
to go for a walk
but not in a circle,
in a line,
with a fresh start
and a clear finish.
I want to go
but I can't remember
where or who
I am,
and I think
I must be dreaming
but I can't remember
what that means.
and now I'm afraid
again,
and the relatives
and the demons
are coming for me
again,
and the house
I'm in,
isn't mine.

a small move toward a simple faith

I have found
a way to get in.
I have found
an opening.
it is small
and inconveniently
located.
it appears to have been
long avoided.
I can think of
many things
that appear this way.
I think I can get
all of myself
through.
I cannot be sure
I am thinking
clearly.
once inside,
I believe
some changes
can be made.
I am unsure
about the lifespan,
of changes
made
in this fashion.
of the many things
I am unsure of,
this takes precedence.
I stumbled upon this,
I do not believe

this weakens it.
there are many things
I do not believe.
if I return,
I hope to have learned
something about
the nature of my journey.
if I have not,
more than all
will surely
be lost.

Wonder

The molars in my face
hurt with
a soft, dull ache.
I can taste blood
in my mouth.
Can't help but think
of all the PCP
I used to smoke.
I sit in my car
with the sun beating down
on my face.
I'm smoking cigarettes,
something I haven't done
in years,
not that it matters now.
I park in front
of the railroad tracks,
my son always loved trains.
Watching them go by
makes me think of him.
I know I should
turn off the car
but the hum of the engine
relaxes me...
It's been so long since
I felt relaxed.
I keep easing my
foot off the brake pedal,
gently inching
toward the tracks.
I love
the sound of trains.

I wonder where my son
is now?
I wonder where
my wife is?
It feels good to wonder
and not worry
for a change
I know they're safe,
they're not with me.
It's such a
pretty day.

dance

LETS EAT
OURSELVES
LETS PRETEND
WE'RE CAVES
AND LIGHT FIRES
IN OURSELVES
LETS WALK
IN THE DARK
AND TRIP OVER
OURSELVES
LETS BE
OTHER PEOPLE
AND IGNORE
OURSELVES
LETS FUCK AND FEUD
AND BETRAY
OURSELVES
LETS HAVE A WAR
AND ENLIST
OURSELVES
LETS BE
OUR PARENTS
AND REGRET
OURSELVES
LETS BE DEVILS
AND SACRIFICE
OUR KIDS
TO OURSELVES
BUT LETS DANCE
ALONE
LETS DANCE
DANCE ALONE.

recurring

grew four more
eyes last night,
dreaming about
the crickets.
I can see little
hummingbirds
nesting on my
fingertips.
I want to touch you
with them,
so you can feel
their little wings.
I wonder what
other things
these new eyes
will show me.
I can't wait
to go outside.
I wonder what
the night
will look like?
I want to meet
all the beings
I've been
living with
all this time.
I like these eyes.
Crickets really know
what they're doing.
Remind me to tell you
about the eyes I grew
when death accepted

my mother's invitation.
What to do with
all this seeing?
I wonder and wonder
what to do,
what to do.
remind me to tell you
what it was
and who was who.

Good-bi Lili

It was my
sometimes
lesbian
aunt Lili
that taught me
about the clitoris
"...get to know the clit
and women will
love you ...." she said....
she was right.

In a way,
she was more like
an uncle,
but I liked that
about her
because my uncles
were more like
demons
or stepfathers.
She was a black belt
and rode a motorcycle
and had grown
a mustache.
The family
had turned on her
but I never did.
they had
kind of
turned on me
too
but Lili.....

man,
she just
liked me.

Now she has cancer.
I guess she's
had it for
a while
but I never knew.
I guess it's
not something
you advertise.

I wonder how she's doing,
and if death is
coming for her.
she's one
of my favorite aunts.
Twenty years ago,
she found Jesus,
I guess she had been
looking for something
to help her,
something to save her.
But her fanatical
Christianity
took something
from her,
and she wasn't the same
without it.
maybe it wasn't Jesus
that took it?
maybe she thought
Jesus could help her

get it back?
I guess he
helped her alright.
My dad said
she'd had
a double
mastectomy.
I wonder what
the doctors did
with the two breasts
they cut off?
my dad said
the surgery
didn't get all the cancer.
must suck
to lose your breasts
but still keep
the cancer.
It seems certain
she's going to die
real soon,
at least,
that's what
my father said.

I haven't seen her
in years,
but if she dies,
somehow,
I'm really going
to miss her.
really going to regret
never telling her
that I loved her.

Inclement Love

stay close
to the fire
my love,
this storm is flames.
tornadoes tracing paths
along the scars of
your face,
pictures of beauty
dying for me
to get lost in.
I thank you for
this forest of your hair ...
you my terrible
walk in the woods.
this smoke of you
all over my clothes,
in the eye
the eye of the storm.
go if you must,
jump into the abyss,
but take me with you.
everything is fire
these days.
if you're burning
I'm burning with you.
let this love
be our ruin
if ruin is
what life's
to make of us...
tangled up in you
like the rope

that hangs me.
I don't let go
cause the greats
are taking
the big swim in the lake.
I don't let go
even if it means
taking us both down.
I will, I will,
I've shown you
I'm not kidding.
just you and I,
all there ever was
all I've ever wanted,
because the clouds
are your name,
even the big black
ugly ones
that bring the
snarling tongue
of death.
even those
I'll take,
the madness of your eyes
when the light shifts,
I've bled this
I will forever...
I love you,
you are the death of me...
the life of me,
the family of all my
warring selves
rip me to pieces....
that the world may never

beat you to it...
I want you to do it
I want you ....
and me
to stay close
to the fire.
it's where we met
and where
we should end.

old friend (for RSW)

don't look for me
in the wind
or the sand
or the stars.
finding me
will only
lead
you
back
to yourself
and
you don't
want
to go there
believe me...
It's
where I've been
all this time
and I can't
for the life of me
find
my way
back.

as good as any muse

sleep
pulls at my eyes
and I begin
to feel
the sharp
but tiny
bites
of insects,
yet I cannot
pull myself
away....
from the
work
at hand,..
and it is not
some form of
artistic dedication,
nor is it some
fear
of surrender,
but more
a wanting
to know
a bit
more,
before
deciding
to abandon it
completely.
and
although the goal
is vague

and the reward
non-existent,
I feel compelled
nonetheless,
and that
is a little,
better
than nothing.

hollowed out

I see myself get arrested,
over and over
for killing you.
no matter what scenario
I try to super-impose,
the outcome is
always the same:
your blood
on my hands,
and the inevitable
police.
it becomes
this terrible game
I play.
but sometimes
your face changes.
I get confused.
I forget
which particular
you, I'm after.
pedophile?
wife-beater?
deadbeat dad,
adulterer,
coward?
which of you is it?
in the end there are
some things
that don't change.
some things
that always,
remain

the same:
your blood
always red,
your death
always just.
and me,
carried away,
lighter,
and just
as hollow
as ever.

Weakness

don't forget me
in your dreams,
in your
innocent visions
of our future
together.

don't let the
pressure
of my apathy,
bruise
your confidence,
or your
determination.

I know
I am weak
and I need you
to be
strong for me.

I need
you
to be
what you
want
from
me.

Closure

meditating on
the nature of perception
and
the algebra of hope,
when the phone rings.
It's my mother.
she's been
dead for three years
so you can imagine
my surprise.

"listen son.." she says,
"sorry about the suicide,
I just couldn't deal anymore
you know?"
I told her
I knew.

she said
she called
because she'd been
worried
about my diabetes
and all my drinking.
I told her
everything was fine
and that things happened
for a reason.

I told her,
for once
I had everything

under control.

can you believe
that bitch
laughed at me?

It's ok though,
I'm glad she
reached out to me,
I'm glad she was
worried.
but she really
didn't have to,
I've got shit
handled,
and I'm doing
just fine.

my terms

I'm delirious
again,
drank five cans
of beer,
took one
and a half pills,
smoked
a variety
of plants,
all to alter
me into
some other
submission.
a feeble attempt
to paint my chains
another color.

the dissonance
rings,
like screams
humming me to sleep.
smoking only
to breathe in a fire
already
consuming me.
a need to be still
driving me into
the darkest corners.

my mind:
a bad montage
of pleasures

and conquests.
fleeting and fading
into insignificance:
a tired druid
aped into ordinary
and predictable
cages.
scratching and
yawning
into oblivion.

humming
forgotten hymns
and raising
a dented can
to the sky.
a toast to the void.

coming to terms,
again in silence,
again in solitude.
coming to terms
with the ever
present
nothing,
that follows me
everywhere.

Little Graves

When I was little
I used to bury things
in the yard,
out back.
I counted paces
from the graves
to the trees,
from the trees
to the windows,
from the windows
to the doors.
I drew out
maps
with x's
and arrows
and words
in code.
I hid the maps
in secret places
and spoke
to no one
about what
I had done.
It was all
so secretive
and exhilarating.
Every month or
so I would
forget where
one of the maps
lay hidden,
I would forget

the things
I had buried
and wondered
why
I had buried them
at all.
nothing that tangible
exists
for me
anymore.
I look back
on those times
very rarely
and often wonder
what it was
I was doing.
I still
bury things,
thoughts and feelings
mostly,
but I forget
what they are
or where
I hid them,
or why
I felt the need
to bury them
at all.

Re-Creation

fifth and main:
I am looking
for the man,
that looks
like the man,
that tried to
sell me crack
in New Orleans.
I am looking
to score
a handful of pills.
not the blue ones.
I have grown tired
of the blue ones.
I am looking for
the white ones
or the yellow ones
or the ones that look
like rain.
I am looking too hard
and reading too much
into
all the shit I'm seeing.
I am looking for
the white ones
but I know
I will take
damn near anything
he has.
my woman waits
in the car
around the corner.

I know
she is waiting
hard.
she is waiting
for me
to make
the weekend
happen
and I cannot
disappoint her.
not tonight
no, no....
not tonight.

Fine, just fine.

my mother had
recently killed herself
and I had been
quite depressed.
my wife worried
my depression
might
drag her down
as well.
she thought
it would be
good for the
two of us
if she left
for the weekend
to Las Vegas,
with some friends.
all her friends
were male,
of course.
she thought
the solitude
might do me
some good.
so I stayed home,
to type.
after the third beer
I began to curse her,
silently
in my head.
after the fifth
I cursed aloud.

I began imagining her
laughing and drinking
with all those men.
at first, I was angry
but slowly
It became
something else.
soon,
I began imagining
different scenarios,
in which I'd be informed
of her
untimely death:
car crash,
overdose,
falling off a roof
drunk.
in each one,
I took the news
remarkably well.
always calm
and composed.
helpfully answering
the police's questions.
without a single
moment
of terror.
this began
to soften
my mood.
soon
the poems began
to roll on out.
really solid lines,

with power
and grace.
I began to feel
strong again,
a sense of purpose
began to form.
I really thought
I had put
all of her
behind me,
when the phone rang
bringing her
suddenly
back.
she said
she called
to see
how I
was
doing.

bait and trap

the plan
is to catch them
when they don't know
they're listening.
feed them
in the dark,
when they don't know
they starve.
the plan is to lure them
with the hope of glory.
tempt their captivity
with the thrill of freedom.
but nothing ever goes,
according to plan.
I am ready
for that too.
I have an alternate
but I am not
telling you.
you could be
one of
them.
and the plan
is to catch
all of you
off guard.

four one four

there was a note
on the door,
something about
the rent.
I was too high
to figure it out.
I went inside
the tiny room.
I stared
at the eight foot
wooden crucifix
RSW
had made me.
I stared
at the seven foot
stage-prop
coffin
Carol
had given me.
it was
too bad
no one knew
how cool I was.
I lit
a cigarette
and wondered
why
I didn't have
any company,
wondered
where
they would sit

if I did.
it was a small room,
too small
for even me.
I got up
flicked my cigarette
out the one
window
and left,
locking
the door
behind me.
I decided
it was time
for people
to learn.

American Hotel

hot ash
down the front
of my red shirt.
high heels
laying on their side
by my window sill.
some dream
floating
softly up
toward the ceiling,
lit cigarette
resting
on the edge
of the ashtray.
the future
will not come here,
does not want
that kind
of exposure.
I leave
the front door
open to the public.
it is the only
door.
I fear cages.
my chair
faces the window,
away
from the door.
the window
faces a brick wall
across the street.

there are windows
in between
some of the bricks.
sometimes
I see people
behind them
but they never
see me.
they aren't looking
for anything.
they have found
everything
they will ever
need.
they are not
my people.
I don't have any,
this is alright.
there are worse
things
than not having
any people
of your own.
I can hear my neighbors
down the hall.
all of their doors
are closed,
but I can still hear them.
no one leaves
their doors open.
the way it
should be.
I am glad about this.
I don't want to see them

accidentally,
while walking
to the bathroom
down the hall.
I wonder what they eat?
the halls never smell
of food or cooking.
I don't like
it here.
I made a mistake
coming here.
there doesn't seem to be
a way out.
I have become
a part of something
here,
I don't like whatever
it is,
but it intrigues me.
I could ponder it forever.
I think I will,
there doesn't seem to be
anything else to do.
I put out my cigarette
and light another.
it's 2:30
Sunday afternoon.
it doesn't feel
like Sunday,
it never does anymore.
it never feels like
anything.

Suggestion Box

I am not
this empty,
not as dark
nor as cold.
it is only my flame
put to sleep too soon.
it is only my seeing,
glancing away.
do not judge my eyes
for their lack of fire.
it has not always
been this way,
I too wrestled destiny
to her knees,
I too sang Pandora
turbulent songs.
but the nights
brought
fancy promises,
of more and more,
and I whored
at the thought
of a never-ending
rise.
but to look
at me now
is to see
a puddle,
content
in its stillness.
to look at me now
is to cradle

yesterday's
glory.
but I am not
as barren
as this,
only more
and more
open
to suggestion.

strangers

I have a picture
of my mother
in my wallet.
she is
very young in it.
I never knew her
to look
so young.
I may have taken that
away from her,
among other things.
I have trouble putting
other photos
in my wallet
now.
none seem
appropriate.
I think maybe
I should take
my mother
out,
but then I remember
that death
already has.
and the feeling
I get now
is not sadness
like before,
it is something else.
sometimes
I find myself
on the toilet

without
something to read.
it's at times like these
that I take out
my wallet
and look
at the woman
in the black and
white
photo,
realizing,
I don't recognize her.
I don't even
know her...
and now,
I never will.

meaning

my muscles are weak
and my flesh sags,
weighted down
by the fat
I've grown
over
years of abuse
and neglect.
I resent my body
for not
overpowering
my brain.
I ache for revolution
but lack
a leader.
I have never been
much more
than a
follower.
the thought
fills me
with shame and
self-loathing.
even now
I drain beer
as opposed
to making
just one move
toward a change.
sickened by
my own
inevitability

my mother died
in vain.
I have learned
nothing
from her death,
but the simple fact
that death
can be
as meaningless
as life is
pointless.

Death Trip

the contemplation
of death
is like masturbating
to the thought
of yourself
masturbating.
yet it is probably
as old
as death itself.
I, of course,
would rather contemplate
the birth
of the rice noodle
or the
passing of wind.
but such choices
never seem
to be up
to me.
if they were,
I would
not be writing this
now.
if they were,
I would not
be writing
at all.
in other words:
it is death
that's to blame
for this
mediocre poem.

Legacy

whenever placed
in front of
a microphone,
I can never
resist
the urge
to scream.
I find it
necessary.
and although
it may
be considered
improper
form,
I can never
seem
to tone it
down.
perhaps
long after
I am dead
and gone,
the scream
will be all
they will
remember,
and that
of course
is fine
with me.

III

please, don't misunderstand

Every time she comes over I tense up a bit. It's not her. It's what's in her bra. She always carries baggies of meth in her bra. She's always high on meth. I can't remember what she looks like when she's not high. I imagine she might look tired or relaxed, it's been too long to remember it clearly. Don't get me wrong, it's not like there's a problem or anything, it's just that, well ...I've done meth with her sometimes, but I don't like to all the time. Sometimes it's just not the right time. But there's always that moment that eye thing. You know, she'll look over, I'll look back The invitation just hanging in the air and then it's all on me and believe me, I'm not the kind of person that should be left to make those kinds of decisions. I usually just avoid any prolonged eye contact until I'm sure I know what the best thing to do is. You don't want to let her catch your eyes until you're sure what the best thing to do is. It could be a trap. There's a kind of strength involved that needs to be built up. It's not instinctual, you must summon it first. Last time I was caught off guard I was up for three days. You might think that exciting in some way, and for the first two days it was. But that third fucking day. Jesus. I felt as if my internal organs were swelling and threatening to burst out of my skin. I could not stop sweating. I was having palpitations which frightened me. I think the fear was making me sweat and the sweat, in turn, was making me more afraid. It's that kind of cycle I really don't want any part of, but I never remember that at the appropriate time. Not till it's too late. You know when too late is. Well she came by last night but I, well I didn't, you know so everything worked out alright But don't think I didn't consider it. And please don't misunderstand, I mean I really do love her but that thing in her bra is just. ....overwhelming I guess is what I mean. I got past it okay and I don't want you to worry because I really am fine. But well, she said hi and wants you to call her and I just thought I should warn you that her bra is full and she's in a bad way and I think she might have a little crush so be careful okay? Just be careful with her.

only god

believe though
the current
apathy,
preaches otherwise.
repent
though the masses
condone consent.
the light dims
in soft response
to an
insistent dark.
the worms
swim
the earth
toward
death.
the rain
beckons,
the hollowed
to drown.
Rise though
the devout
expect you
to fall.
you are
your own
savior.
you are
the only
god
you will ever
need.

hard up

I have drunk
and caroused
with the best of them:
poets, painters,
photographers
and dancers.
I have heard stories
that changed my life,
and I have forgotten
almost all of them.
I have kissed women,
and touched girls.
I have seen the stars
after falling heavily
to the ground.
I have slept in the hell
of a flute player's despair.
I have seen women
walking naked
down the hall.
I have hopped
into backs of cars
not knowing
where I was headed
and smiled
when we finally
got there.
I have eaten,
drank,
and vomited
all within
an amplified

minute.
I have been
to parties
that resembled
blood rituals,
and I have left them
without saying
goodbye
I have done all this
but am
Still empty,
stupid,
and
always
hard up
for more
and more
action.

safety net

she turns eyes
with the whites
gone raspberry-red,
and asks me
for a light,
using up the last
of what was left
of her coherence.
I light her
and wonder
if she's still
taking pills
as she inhales,
sucking
more
than the smoke,
exhaling plumes
that curl
around
the greasy strings
of her hair.
and she takes
what could have been
a deep and longing look
into my eyes,
her gaze
landing somewhere
beneath my chin.
I slither down
in my chair
to help her look
along

but we miss
each other
completely
and everything is
as it should be.
I am so glad
that I married her,
so that every time
she slips
I can always be
there
to catch her.

wishing won't make it so

I don't want
to hear
how tragic
and sad
it all is,
how shocking
and
out of the
blue.
I don't want
to hear
about how well
I seem
to be
taking it.
I am not
taking
it,
it
is taking me.
she is dead.
she killed
herself.
she chose.
end of
fucking
story,
and it is
really
fucked up.
so much more
than sad.

she could be
burning in hell,
if there is a hell.
how am I
supposed
to deal
with that?
I guess
that's just
it.
there is no:
dealing with it,
there's just
living with it.
I wish
there was
more
but there isn't.

pass

I have retained
much more
than I can hold,
seen beyond
what I wanted to see
and touched
what I
would never
embrace.
I have seen
the devil's face
in mine,
and searched for what
I left behind.
in the pockets
of trashed dreams,
in the clouds
of forgotten skies.
I am tired
and I want out.
no more:
demons
in the faces
of friends.
no more:
nights
sweating out
the black urges.
no more: ultimate truths,
no more: breathing walls,
no more: cigarettes
at dawn,

no more: waiting
for the fucking come-on.
I have been there.
it is late
and I really
should be
getting back.
thanks for
the invite
though,
thanks for
trying to show me
what you thought
I should see,
but I've seen it
and, don't get me
wrong,
it was great but,
you go ahead
you'll love it.
call me when
you
get back.
can't wait
to hear
all about it.

dark inside

deep into
the groove
of the slit wrist,
I shake with
enough anger
to start a war
and justify
the bloodshed.
I walk hard,
trying to hurt
the street
and invite
any motherfucker
to even try
looking at me
wrong.
the bad days
mount
and multiply
into weeks
and months,
and I cannot
be pacified.
fuck the pigs
and their panic,
fuck the hypes
and the drunks,
the whores
and the idiots.
there is just me
and my fat
and a tight

white
ball
of seething.
don't look at me.
I will not
see you,
don't want
to be seen.
there is just me
and death
and the black space
in between.
don't try to
know me,
I am dark inside
but I will eat
your light
like a cannibal.
stay away
from me,
keep your distance,
you don't know me
or what I might
be capable of.

wrong turn

you thought
you'd
just step back
and watch
for a while.
you thought
everyone
would just wait
for your demons
to lose interest
bored by the
wayward
turn
of your
ambition.
oh but you
lost interest too.
and something barren
spoke to you
in the dark.
something
pitiful,
flattered you there.
and you were
cheapened
and fattened
loosened
and scattered.
fed
and led
to believe
that all

the others like you,
were right.
so you
made promises
to the night.
and no one
listened,
no one
cared,
and you aimed
your perceptions
elsewhere,
never picturing
the end.
and in your mind
you never
got there.
in your mind,
you never left.

climbing & falling

don't want
to get up
for work.
want to
fuck up my hair,
sleep late,
drink hard,
and create
like the end
of the world
were as near
as it seems.
want to sing
a dying man
a song
that sends him
on his way,
want to feel
something
when I pray.
don't want
to need
to go to work
today.
I used to believe
in things,
speak
with conviction.
I used to shine
when rubbed
the right way,
but that was

in the past
before I started
trying to climb.
before I knew
how far
I'd fallen.
It's too bad
because
I do have
some vacation
days
left.

Eye to I

if I could put
my heart
through this wall,
if I could
hit you with it,
bludgeon
something
to death
with it,
I would.
if I could
work it out
enough
to hate
with indifference:
hate puppies,
babies,
grandmas,
and god,
I would,
but I can't,
not with
indifference.
and it slows me down.
too many feelings,
too much nuance.
and so this bottle
keeps her eye,
and I,
in turn,
misdirect
mine.

from the POND, to the OCEAN
(for Angelo Moore)

I heard his band,
was falling apart.
I heard he was
smoking crack.
I heard there were
very few
original members
left in the group.
very few
of them
was
more
than enough.
when the songs
were over,
I knew
they had lost
nothing.
I knew
they had
little
left to lose.
fish
are tougher
than men,
so to the naysayers
I say: learn to
swim fuckers,
learn to swim.

fair

death
took my hand
and told me
she loved me.
I asked her
about my mother,
and she told me
not to worry,
'all things
come,..
and go
as they should'.
so I looked
and looked
in my pockets
for change,
I thought
that death
deserved
a tip.
some compensation
for a thankless
job,
but I was broke
as usual
and had nothing
to offer her.
well, I guess
we can get
square
on the other
side.

dime (for J.)

He is 10,
getting older.
his secrets
are growing.
now he:
hides things
in the fridge,
takes longer
in the shower.
he is 10
and almost
always
on fire,
trying to test
the reach
of his power.
and I can see him
watching me,
looking for answers,
boundaries,
and flaws.
trying to find
some bullshit
on the statue of me
he's supposed to be
looking up to.
he is short
for his age,
though the age
does not belong
to him.
he dreams

of being tall
constantly changing
the pictures
on his wall.
he is 10
and already
beginning to die.
somersaulting
with his destiny
learning to lie,
and hiding his eyes.
next year is junior high
and I am:
drinking beer,
smoking cigarettes,
squinting my eyes
and getting ready.

absence

with father gone
to that other pair
of legs
to swim between,
mom just weeping
along with all
the heavily made-up
'novela' women.
and me just wondering
who's going to stop
my uncles from
kicking my ass?
father gone
with some
Tijuana-whore-waitress
from the local bar,
and mom just
on the phone,
desperate with
cigarettes clenched
between her teeth,
and me only seven
not man enough
for anything.
plotting revenge against
all the fucked up men
I wanted to destroy.
one day they would pay.
I thought and prayed
but nothing happened.
over and over again,
just beaten down

old Normandie avenue,
full of hate and tears.
and everyone saying
what an asshole
my father was
and me just hating
them all for it,
wishing pain on
so many people
I'd lose track.
then mom replaced dad
with a seventeen year old boy.
and they had a daughter
and they had a son
and twenty four years later
my mother killed herself
with an overdose
of pills
designed to keep
her heart
from stopping.
and the only men
I had ever seen
her kiss,
didn't shed a tear
at her funeral.
neither did I,
and I still
don't understand
what any of it
means.
left with nothing.
nothing but tired,
nothing but absence.

big questions

where was god
when you
swallowed
them down?
where was god
when you
changed your mind?
where was he
when your heart just
stopped?
where was I
when you
needed me most?
where did love go,
when the light
began to dim?
when the dark swelled?
where was god
when your children's souls
flashed before you?
where was faith
when your hope
lay herself down
on the cold
hard
tracks?
where is destiny
now?
who keeps her clean?
designs her disguises?
where was your
born-again

sister
when you died?
did you leave happy?
did the angels sing?
did you leave
a promising
future behind?
when do I
begin to heal?
the dogs are howling
and I can feel
your terror
in my teeth,
and I can't wake up
and I can't
make it stop.
and god is nowhere.

chance

eyes dead red
as twilight
rests her head
upon the night,
and the people
scurry
to their hiding
places,
to do their
secret things.
I sleep
but dream
too much
to rest.
dead mothers
and rising
tides: all
too much
to bear.
days hunted
for solace,
only to return
to the cage,
defeated.
sucking dead air
into battered lungs.
eyes dead red,
fat from tears
too proud to
spill.
so many greats
died this way,

but I am not
alone.
only pretend
to be.
failure
upon failure,
upon dis-illusion
dis-appointment
dis-enchantment
dis-association.
I brood,
intending
to glorify
this sorrow,
but it reeks
of fraud
and boredom.
even tragedy fails
to convert it.
leaving only
cowardice
to camouflage
an ordinary ineptitude.
I drink
for lack of something
meaningful
to do.
I drink
in order
to destroy
any
chance.

Sick Leave

so
I tell her
what happened,
the whole
damned
story:
the cops
the base-heads
the porno shop,
the guy
that led me
to the guy
that I actually
scored from,
the way
I got the hell
outta there
and how
I took two
of the pills
as soon as I
got on the bus,
and how high
I was
before I
even got
back home.
"well there you go...." she said,
"now you have something to write about."
of course,
she was wrong.

Cinema Verite

we were going
to the movies,
just as soon
as he was done
making her cry.
she was six,
he was eleven.
I was seven.
he made her
sit on the chair.
told her to
lift her arms
up in front of her.
every time she
lowered an arm,
he hit her.
he hit the arm
she just
couldn't keep up
anymore.
he told her:
"if you scream
I'll hit you harder."
she cried
but never
made a sound.
I was impressed.
she could cry
without
ever
making a sound.
I wanted to be

like her.
I wanted to cry
without
making a sound.
I wanted to be
like my uncle too.
I wanted
to hurt somebody.
not little May,
but somebody,
someday.
after a while
he got bored,
and we went to the movies.
on our way out he told her:
"if you tell anybody what happened,
I'll kill you."
I knew he wouldn't kill her,
but I could tell
she believed him.
I was so impressed.
I wanted to threaten
somebody like that.
so they'd believe me.
I wanted someone
to take *me*
that seriously.
we left her there,
wiping her tears
and snot
on the sleeve of her shirt.
it was really bright outside.
I was in such a good
mood.

it was good to have
my uncle around,
to teach me
how to be a man.
My dad just
couldn't be bothered
he was too busy,
living his life
with
his own people.

for the poets

make your way
in the dark,
the perimeter
is calling.
you have
lingered
in the soft center
far too long,
now you must return,
to where it was
that first
frightened you.
the fear was never
meant
to dissuade you,
but only
to heighten
your senses.
make your way
back to the fringe,
it is where
you were headed,
before
the dead
obscured your path.
know that
their presence
was meant
only to confirm,
the depth
of your journey,
and remember:

it is not
for everyone
to report
from this field,
one has to be
chosen,
as you
have been.
now,
get to work.

making me

you were
making me watch.
first watch,
then participate.
you were making me,
and that made you
the bad one...
you the bad one
not me.
you were making me
promise
never to tell.
you were leading me down
the stairs
to hell,
and I liked
where we were headed.
the secret place
of your insistence.
I liked it there
because I trusted you
at first...
then tried to get away..
because I ran from you,
at first,
then tried
to make you stay.
you were making me
feel,
what I didn't think
I should.
I hate that it was you,

but now know
it had to have been.
I hate that
it was you
that gave up
on it
first.
that gave up
on me
and
left me,
alone,
with the *others*.

Seize the...

stand up today.
brave the wind,
and the dark.
remember the night
your father disappeared,
and how
your mother cried,
the first angry tears
you'd ever seen.
stand up today.
pull
all those broken selves
together.
an entire life,
remains,
to rest and reflect,
but today
you must stand.
stand up to
the rage
and the cowardice.
stand up
to the sting
of all the cuts,
you held
so close.
tomorrow,
you can surrender,
tomorrow
you can sleep.
but today,
try and pull

from all that's
tried to hold you down.
try and
open the doors
you made,
for yourself
to hide behind.
stand up today,
in case the end
of the world
is tomorrow.
hold all your hurt
up to the sun
till it burns,
till it burns.
don't forget
what happened
yesterday.
don't
let it
happen
again.

restoration

gathering up all the
broken pieces of selves.
the shards of me,
the slivers and the chunks.
gathering them,
from the bathroom and the car,
from the mirrors and the bars.
wiping up the blood of me,
scrubbing at my stains,
my brains....all my remains.
wonder how I've gotten myself
so everywhere.... so ...
all over the place.
and none of it looks
like it goes together,
none of me matches..
and I'm dirtier and heavier
than I remember.
because I want to make something
of myself after all,
all those years, so sure
I wanted nothing, so sure I wouldn't
meld....with any of those identities,
now thinking
perhaps I was mistaken,
now thinking perhaps...
all is possible...
gathering up the
shapes and shadows,
the whispers and the rumors,
assembling the timelines
of all those warring lives.

because I want to be on time,
because there's a fight to win..
because there's a reason to....
and I cannot attack
with only fragments,
cannot defend
only portions of me.
cleaning up the spill
of all my sacred notions,
because I believe in them again...
because I want more than
just my faith restored.

Inheritance Annulled

dad your eyes
were dead.
did I ever tell you that?
all the dead rage and hot fire
you spewed.
dad I can't tell you,
how hard I was listening.
I liked the way
you would wrap the belt
around your fist.
tight and powerful,
knowing nothing I could do,
could make it slip.

strange when you left
to sleep with
someone else's mother.
strange when you left
to raise
someone else's sons.
watching them
from a distance,
as they grew hateful
and proud.
just like you daddy,
just like you.
I wanted
to be strong
like them.
to belong,
like them.
but I didn't

and I couldn't.
strange
how you reacted,
when their fists
cut into my face.
how your eyes were dead
and you were
so proud of them
for hating me
as much as you did.
I could see it
in your eyes.
you wouldn't believe
how hard,
I looked into your eyes.
those pretend brothers,
those better-for-you sons,
so many years later:
all ex-military,
all of them cops.

I remember at grandma's birthday,
how they gravitated towards me and
laid their guns across the table,
they were so proud and hateful,
I thought:
you did this dad,
you did this.
and I was so relieved,
you abandoned me
like you did.
I understood then
that you were a kind of poison.
suddenly

it was so clear,
why I had always
been,
so obsessed with death.
it was
because of you dad,
because of you.

so I wanted to
thank you dad,
thank you
for hating me
enough
to save me,
from all
you had
to give.

adversary poem #8

who do you
think
you are?
I'll tell you:
you are
a cluster of cells,
fucked
into being.
two wrongs fusing,
to jettison you
here.
a bad idea
made form.
everything you say
is a testament to this.
you are
a walking,
talking,
human repellant.
a constant reminder,
of what
not to be.
this is why
I hold you
so close.
this is why
I keep you here.
not quite
a penance
but more
a reminder:
that the adversary

is real
and walking
next to me
every day.
so say something,
please.
attack
and
attack me.
I can take it.
give it to me,
let me have it.
I need all of it
to make me
strong enough
to love you.

the one, true god

Shall open his mouth
and spill his wrath
upon the world
into the
bleeding ears
of man
with a message of
disappointment
and vengeance.
It will be
seriously
fucked up
for everyone.
at least
that's
what I've
been hearing.

today

it's been a long day.
I didn't know
you were going to die
when I woke up
this morning.
explains why I
was so irritated
in the shower.
now there doesn't seem
to be a point
to being irritated
anymore.
lots of things
don't have a point
now.
I hope
I can get to sleep..
never hoped
for something
so hard
in my life.
and that's sad,
I should have hoped
that you'd live
longer.
but that's the thing,
I didn't know
you were going
to die
today.

revelation

I open myself up,
the blade just one
rusted
recollection.
I do it right
down the middle.
the belly splits easily,
a leakage dripping
down the sides,
like some bad
stigmata.
but amidst all the stink
of entrails and gluttony,
I find no sign
of the tapeworm.
I lift flaps of flesh
and ropes of matter
but still....
no sign.
I was so sure
I could feel it moving,
feeding on the blood
of all my bad impulses.
but if there's no worm
then what could be
moving in there?
after hollowing myself
completely out...
I become convinced
the worm has died
and I've already
passed it.

so I
make a mental note
to take a closer look at
what passes through
before I flush.
because without a worm
there is only me,
and that just
will not
do.

hang 'em high

flags unfurling,
burning, taunting dogs,
snapping and howling.
flag for saluting,
a weak allegiance
steeped in blood.
flags finding
their way home,
in the trunks of cars,
in the gagged mouths
of weeping rapes,
and lipstick smears.
flags braided
into ropes,
fashioned into nooses.
blindfold flags,
panty flags
flags of mops
flags of skin,

and the walk
to the border
always:
long to get out
longer to get in.

flags of hoods,
flags of bags over our heads,
around our bodies.
eyes and eyes
looking up
at the symbols

of our divides.
so hang em high
and let them billow,
all emblems
and colors,
dancing and aligning,
with all our generals,
our butchers,
decorated and
bathed
in all
our blood.

permanent

not with
all the books read
and forgotten.
not with
all the epiphanies,
enlightening
then fading...
not with love, eternal,
not with success,
or popularity.... not even
with fame....
but only with
fire and death
and trauma.
only then
can you
be assured
of real and
permanent
change.
even
god
would have.
told you that,
if you'd had
sense enough
to put
more screaming
into your prayers.

Interpret This

I dream that I'm driving to work,
but it's the middle of the night,
and I'm wearing shorts
and smoking crack in the car.
I dream I'm at a party
and some woman I've never seen
is trying to shake her tits into my mouth,
but I can never get them in there
just too busy turning my head
this way and that way,
looking for my wife or my boss
or my beer or my father.
I dream I can see my mother's corpse
lying naked on a table near a window
with white curtains and beautiful light
streaming into the room.
I dream her body to look like a giant balloon
of super-thin skin, I touch it and it deflates
all thin skin rippling, down the sides of the table.
I dream of climbing up there and pulling my
mother's deflated corpse over me like a blanket,
struggling to keep her from falling to the floor,
because I don't want her to fall, not on the floor.
I dream of driving in circles in downtown nowhere,
lost and afraid that I won't find the guy that'll sell me
the shit that I'm after. I dream it's the middle of the
night, most of my dreaming always happens in the
middle of the night. I dream of being choked to
death...I dream of dying.. sometimes I'm falling,
sometimes drowning.. sometimes just suddenly
collapsing....I sometimes dream that I'm learning
everything it was I was trying to learn,

but I can never remember it when I wake up.
I wonder if that's why people, sometimes
don't want to wake up.....why people,
sometimes....choose to sleep forever.
in my dreams: I'm always lost, wrong and
out of context. there are always strangers
and puzzles and a feeling of quickly approaching
derangement and madness. the places are always
foreign yet familiar and the mood is always urgent or
dangerous. Even when I dream of sex there is always
something wrong, and I am always going crazy.
sometimes my dream-feelings
follow me into my waking self ....
that happened more frequently
when I was smoking pcp,
lately I've been thinking
more and more about pcp,
and dreaming and dying and going crazy.
though I get the feeling that going crazy
is not actually somewhere you go, but rather
somewhere you remember
having always been from.

this way

NOW:

with your lipstick smeared,
the dark one,
the one that looks like blood...
smeared not like you were kissing
but more like
you were wiping something
from your mouth.....
because you got something
in your mouth...

THEN:

with your dark eye shadow
smeared...
not like you were crying,
but more like
you were running,
and screaming
because something was AFTER you
and you ran so fast, you got all sweaty
and your eyes went red and they
were burning and burning
from looking over your shoulder

NOW:

with your stockings ripping at the toes
from dancing and grinding
in those spiked heels that hurt your feet
but make you feel real dirty

NOW:

with the pain on your face,
biting at your lips
like their meat wasn't yours,
and your tongue flicking and licking,
like you were pressed against someone
and your lipstick smearing, the dark one
the one that looks like blood
and your eyes...like two black holes
sucking the light out of the stars

THEN :

with your toes curling,
clawing at the carpet
as you crawl and crawl
like a hungry panther
digging your nails in,
gripping and bracing for something...
something that's coming for you
something you want
but are still afraid of.. closing your eyes
as if to get a clearer picture of it...

THEN:

me with my hands
speaking in tongues
along your legs,
parting the seas
of all your secrets,
fingering my way into
the hungry dark

of all your yearning,
pushing and pinning you
down, further and further down
and your pulse beginning to quicken,
an animal trapped in your fluttering eyes,
my name slipping and slipping
from your lips. with you cursing and pleading and
finally beckoning, from your belly
to your back, then on your side,
tying your wrists and
binding your ankles
the gentle straps
to keep you still
removing your choice
and your lips moving,
mumbling as if to pray,
all the things
you dare not say
I need you this way
tense and restrained
obliged to obey
I need you this way
this way, now.

legion of you

your mouths all
snapping traps
and bottomless wells,
spouting tricky words
with multiple meanings,
and smiles and tears
shifting and changing
like mushroom mirrors.
no light in the
dead pools of
legion eyes.
all that I suspected
more than true.
turning away from
your face,
the final stance toward
a preferred atheism.
a quiet surrender of faith
more bearable
than the obvious alternative.
the legion of you
existing somewhere,
more than here...
being more than this
believing you're affecting
so much more than me.
choosing a barren,
godless plane
over the stink of your
spirit fields burning;
into the future
and back into the past.

knowing I flirted
with all your light,
only to find
I preferred the fire.

church of ME

I hope my grandmother
is burning in hell
for all she did
to my mother
when she was alive.
I hope my uncle Oldemar
falls off his medication,
and finally lets
the demons
eat him.
I'd love to see him
come for his brothers.
I hope,
despite all
I've learned,
because
conditioned response
is more
powerful
than love,
or enlightenment.
tomorrow
I'll get up early,
even though
I want
to sleep
late into the day,
and I'll take
my wife
and son
to breakfast.
rising up

against
the pain,
of another night,
wrestled down
with liquor
and pills.
because
I want to
champion
the causes
no one valued
but me.
because
I'm the only
god,
that
hasn't
failed me.
I'm the only
GOD
I haven't lost
faith in...
so please
if you must pray
pray *to me...*
hail me,
praise ME.
for **I am:**
the truth
the light
and
the way.

IV

Alternative

I used to smoke pcp until I couldn't remember my name or what kind of creature I was or what existence meant. I thought I was peeling back the fabric of the world and that one day I'd be up there with the big ones like Dostoevsky or Nietzsche or even Bukowski. Sometimes I'd roll around in the grass or on the sidewalk or sometimes I'd crawl on top of the roof of some car and just wait for the big answers to come. I would walk around with a vial in one pocket and a pack of cigarettes in the other. I would dip a cigarette in the murky liquid and smoke myself into oblivion. I had a few guys that would follow me around cause they knew I was always holding. I pretended they were friends of mine. you knew the shit was good if you couldn't talk after the first hit. you called that shit : the bomb
There is this strange feeling that washes over when you lose your ability to speak. I used to pretend I was a German Shepherd, fully aware of the stupidity of humanity but unable to articulate it. These sounds would escape in place of words....like some kind of James Brown meets orangutan. Sometimes it would take three hours before consciousness would return. And the process would be so slow, that I would remember who I was by degrees, first living, then human, then my name...then night or day....then finally what time it might be.
It seems juvenile now, but I really did believe I was onto something. I remember having entire conversations with the beings I would encounter on the other side. All my desperate attempts to get them down on paper. The ideas I thought would heal the

world. What did I retain? Brain damage. That's what. But I don't regret it because my memories of that place still beat most memories of this place. they would have beat them all if I'd never met you, but I did and that's why I stopped. You were the only alternative that was worth it. So thanks, thanks for being more than I deserved.

keys

off the vicodin again,
back on the scotch.
took four days to kick,
ten to convince myself,
the timing was right.
pictures are peeling
off of everything...
I'm always so concerned
about the way
I'm seeing.
So much time
and effort wasted,
changing my perspective.
Some days,
I just wait and wait,
for a chance
to close my eyes.
I catch a glimpse
of myself in the mirror,
(I look bad)
and look away.
Sifting through old photos,
trying to bring
my mother...
back to life.
my coke guy
has ecstasy now.
I go back and forth,
almost calling him
for three whole hours.
I wait for the sun
to go down,

then I turn off my phone.
off the vicodin,
back on the scotch.
my aunt puts up
this random photo
on facebook,
the caption reads:
"two months before we lost her,
and she was looking so good."
I throw this heavy book
I haven't written,
through a mirror in my head.
how many other people
do I know that are dead?
I count: one, two
four, six?
I stop counting and start
trying to remember,
how many people
I love that
are still alive:
one, two
seven, twelve?
I stop counting.
off the vicodin,
back on the scotch.
quit smoking
two years ago,
quit crystal meth,
four years ago.
my coke guy,
that sells E now,
called me today to say,
he's selling crystal again,

and this time it's better
and stronger than before.
It's exactly
what I'm hoping, I am
right now:
better *and* stronger
than before.
digging around the
little stashes, in my desk.
I come across some hash
Fat-Hed had brought over
for my birthday.
I crumble some over
the weed in the pipe
and pull at it hard.
as drunk as I am,
I can still think
of two heads
I'd like to hold
underwater.
...and I really want
the scotch..
to help...
grabbing the
fifth beer,
pouring the
third scotch,
and looking
for my car keys.

self-made monster.

the things
that come for you,
your brave attempts
to face them squarely.
and then you're:
overpowered,
taken over,
made weak
and afraid.
so you
learn to hide,
but the things keep
coming,
and finding
where you've hidden,
so you
learn
to hide
inside.
soon the things have you
by the heart,
and even as
they have their way
with whatever
part of you
they choose
to destroy,
you feel removed,
as if
it were a dream
or a scary movie
you must have seen.

but after years and years
of hiding and believing
you weren't affected,
you start to feel safe
and decide to emerge
for just a second,
to test the waters and
brave the wind,
only to find
you've hidden
so well
for so
goddamn long,
even you
can't find
where it is
you've gone.
but don't worry
it's better this way
because honestly
you don't want
to see
what happened to you
while you were away.
you don't want to know
what
you've become,
because I know,
and want you,
to stay
away
from me.

sitting in a chair

pushing myself back
into where I think,
I come from.
and it's dark in there.
heart made heavy by
dead mother's entrails.
looking for A Razor
to match her pills.
looking for a mask to pull over
her green, dead, face.
running from the
hospital again.
running from the
torture doctors,
in that dream, again.
I can feel myself plotting,
but how do I match
it's evil? it's dark?
sitting in a chair,
waiting for the
night to fall,
waiting for the
grass to die.
draining the beer,
draining the scotch,
hoping for just
one good night
of sleep.
how could her jaws
lock up like that?
did she die screaming?
or vomiting?

or both?
I look in the fridge
for something
to put
in the freezer.
tonight
it's the orange juice.
I can't wait
for tomorrow,
to see how much
it's changed.
I wish I could
put myself
in the freezer.
I wish I
could change.

thanks for stopping by

just tell them
I came down
with something,
tell them
I haven't been well.
you can mention my mom,
or my situation at work.
everyone knows
I've been having trouble
with my knee,
and my ankle.
tell them I'm just no good
in social situations.
apologize for me,
for missing:
the funeral,
the baby shower
and little Andy's
birthday party.
tell them
I really wanted to be there.
but you have to
make it
sound convincing,
everyone knows I'm a liar
but I don't want them
to think
I'm an asshole too.
I really do
love everyone,
and really am sorry
for missing everything.

it's just that I can't...
seem..
to get up from here.
and I'm afraid
to go out there.
every time I do,
I bring something
back with me.
it gets on my clothes,
and in my hair.
I don't want that.
I don't want to
get it on me,
and I don't
want it in my house.
and it's for this
reason
that
I'm going to
have to
ask *you*
to leave now.
it's just that
I know
some of it
is on you
and you're getting it
everywhere.
and I can't have that.
soooo.....
thanks for stopping by.
I love you
but
goodbye.

recently passed.

dead,
like a spotted
fish,
all bellied up,
and foggy-eyed.
dead,
like post mortem,
bloated,
ready to pop,
and stink,
and spill
over
the edge of the
aluminum table.
dead,
like the road kill,
baking in the sun.
an opera of finality,
screaming desperately
toward an epic
hush. dead
like the innocent
dreams of youth.
dead,
like a fading
wish upon a star.
no:
natural order
of things.
no:
it's probably
all

for the best.
no:
god has his
reasons.
just dead. simple
and terrible,
quiet
and uneventful.
no : goodbye
no : always alive
in my heart,
no : pseudo sermon
of all this too
shall pass
like the leaves
fucking falling
from the trees,
she's just dead.
dead because
she died.
ok?

metamorphosis

the holes in my head
my eyes keep crawling into,
the desperate escaping
from one bad dream
after another after another....
always driving, or getting high,
or looking for a room
in a building I can never remember.
I used to write them down,
I don't anymore.
all this trouble walking lately.
first my knee, then my ankle,
now my toes,
it's as if the pain is after me,
trying to stop me from
getting where I'm going.
but I don't know where I'm going,
so why is it trying to stop me?
I feel this strange momentum
building, like a swell in my chest.
I mistake it for pain...
I think: my heart is stopping.
my blood is turning.
I think myself into
a quiet panic.
bouncing and limping along
like a coiled spring.
wondering when I'll suddenly
leap out of my skin and just
become already.
become whatever
it is I'm turning into.

4th floor window university

I sat there,
by the window,
drinking beer
smoking cigarettes,
looking down
into the street.
not going anywhere,
not doing anything,
for days,
weeks, months...
flicking the ashes
off my shirt
and wondering
why I bothered,
no one
was coming
to see
my shirt.
every now and again
some happy people
walking down there
would look up
and catch
a glimpse of me,
but then they would quickly
look back down.
they knew
what I had
come there
to learn:
that I was someone
simply

not to be
considered.
to think
that back then,
the idea actually
made me sad.
to think that
there was a time
I believed
that mattered.
I know
better now.
my mistake
had always been
and will
always be....
looking down
and out,
instead of
looking
up
and
in.

the rest of me

my eyes in love.
the temptress wind
pulling
and pulling me
toward
the ledge.
the dead
weight of being
lulling me
to drown.
if only
a still lake
would materialize
before me,
with black water
dark as all
my seeing.
if only
my fatigue could
stop
my breathing.
but it doesn't
as something
in me continues
to survive,
sharpening its teeth
and waiting for
the rest of me
to rise.

Jury Duty

as the witness stammered on ...
contradicting himself
as he struggled through
the defense attorney's
complicated questions,
my eyes grew tired
and fell softly
on the accused,
and then,
as if he felt me
watching him,
he slowly turned
toward me....
sixth seat
out of twelve,
and we looked at each other
fully aware of our
intimate connection.
and I thought about
18th street,
as I read the
roman numerals
tattooed above his eyebrows,
knowing then that he had
committed,
the murder in question.
knowing then we'd never
be able
to convict him.
because the witness
was an idiot and a liar.
my uncle Boris

had been from
18th street,
but his homeboy
killed him
for trying
to
leave the life.
after much
deliberation
we, the jury
found the defendant
innocent.
the prosecution
was very upset.
I was just glad
I got to take
a few weeks
off from work.
Turns out
becoming a U.S.
citizen
really did
have its perks.
God Bless America.

transcendence

It's difficult when you
push up
against the boundaries
so often and so insistently
that you almost
don't expect
to break through,
so that when you do,
you don't know
that you have,
and everything seems
as normal as ever.
but then
something will happen,
some little thing,
a gesture...
a sound,
a vague flickering,
and suddenly
you know,
and then
the question
becomes:
how long have I been here?
and why didn't I notice
the difference between
here
and there?
but you know why
don't you?

untitled paranoia rant #73

I've been avoiding things
made of paper
and when the women
move past me,
I've been turning my head away,
because their power is increasing
and they know it and their eyes
are like bottomless wells that
pull my weakness
into their deep dark.
and me like paper:
just too open to suggestion,
too brimming with possibility,
so I've been avoiding it
like I do my intuition,
because of my fear
of that condition
where you over analyze away
all the meaning
of your experiences.
I am having trouble
digesting meat again and I cannot defecate
without looking down to investigate the stool
because I believe it continues to move
after it exits my body like the worms
that slither out of the eyeless sockets
in my dead mother's head,
that bobs and nods her disappointment
from beyond the grave.
I can see the head of Christ
behind the butcher's apron
that the priest wears,

when I dream that dream
of the apocalypse,
where the lake of fire
is a river and an ocean
and a continent
and a pulsing vulva spilling
blood and lava onto the heads of children,
and the rapture splits the sky
with angels and demons swarm down to fight
and all the Christians don't rise like the prophecy
said they would,
they just stop moving and lie down
and start dying and rotting in the
heat from the flames
that come up out of the cracks
in the sidewalk.
I'm having trouble chewing
and swallowing.
I can't eat eggs anymore
because the yolk hangs on my tongue
like a menstruation
of embryo and darkness,
and I can feel the weight
of death in my food
when I eat,
feel the fear
of the animals and hear the cleavers
and my stomach turns
like there's worms in there,
and I drink and I drink
to stop my head from
playing pictures that
tell stories I don't believe.
I go outside

and make my way
through the crowds of
people
careful to avoid
brushing up against the women
because their power
is increasing and they know
that I can feel it and
they harness it like the rivers
harness the rain,
and I just want
to get more meaning,
because I want to be
more about meaning... and I don't
know what that means but
I want to get it down on paper
but the paper
is just too
open to suggestion and I don't like things
that are too open,
like my heart or my mind
I just want things to be closed...
like the bible or my father's heart
but nothing closes... nothing ends
and perhaps
there isn't an end, but if there isn't then
what happens when I can
no longer continue? what if ... I can't
what if it never....what if I don't....what if...this
just never....

breathing in

my eyes twitching like
cockroach legs,
pointing up toward the sky,
some final indication
that all horrors,
like all hopes,
reach for the sun ....
and burn.
so many memories
hanging by
threads of quiet and
lonely desperation.
I open my eyes
slow and cautious,
fully aware of all the
frightening possibilities.
fearing death
but hurting for its
awful quiet.
no room left
for wonder,
no heart
left for love.
listening
to my own
lies...
believing and living
my ornate fictions,
breathing in
my own
toxic air,
and choking.

The Club

Father's day today,
thinking about
my father and
my mother,
who spread her legs
for all
he was worth.
it's still
very early.
my wife's asleep
and my son is away.
my father is in
another country.
and my mother,
well... she's only
in my memories
now...and not
spreading it
for anyone.
It's a strange feeling
knowing
I'm in this club now.
I've joined the fathers.
and for the first time.....
I'm not afraid,
and I know my son
is on his way
home.

Trick

I've started losing teeth.
It began
a few years ago.
first, just
a couple of molars
in the back,
now,
closer to the front.
I remember when I was twenty,
smoking a lot of pcp
and snorting a lot of speed,
people used to tell me:
that shit is really bad
for your teeth,
and I always thought:
I'll be dead before
that ever becomes
a problem.
but here I am now,
45 years old,
frankly amazed
and almost
disappointed.
It just seemed like
an early,
violent death,
would have been
more appropriate.
the cosmos, it seems,
saw it differently.
the irony does not escape me,
as I rattle on

whistling between
the newfound
holes in my face.
now, when I begin
to tell a story
or ask someone a simple question:
spittle often shoots
out of my mouth.
now when something
strikes me as funny,
I suddenly become
embarrassed to laugh,
for fear of being
seen as more deformed
than I had always imagined.
it's this kind of symbolism
that compels me.
it's this kind of justice
that convinces me.
and as I turn
away from the mirror,
I can't help but smile,
despite the
obvious revelation:
that death,
disguised
as life,
has tricked
me
once again.
that bitch.

surrender

my shoulders:
slumped and defeated,
as the last
of the good memories
float away.
the dark settles in
like an old friend
come to spend the night,
as my tired eyes
gently close,
2 little doors pushing up
against the cold.
thoughts of death,
and spots of blood,
making patterns,
on my eyelids.
sleep beckoning
and teasing,
like a pretty girl…
just close enough
to be
completely
out of reach.
I give in
knowing
that nothing
will come
of my surrender.
wondering what
a revolution
might bring.
wondering

but knowing,
the fight
has left me.

me beast

again,
it is fed,
again
it sleeps,
comfortable
and smiling.
as I lie awake
in bed ...
blaming the pillows,
or my muscles...
or the temperature
of the moon.
as if blame could
ever keep it
from eating me alive.
and I know
it's the reason
I spring up
from sleep,
despite the dreams
I try to accuse.
and as I lay there,
contemplating rest
or the coming of the dawn,
I always feign surprise
when it rises,
to look me dead
in the eyes....
as if surprise
could ever mask
the intimacy
of our exchange.

spreading disease

something turning
in the eyes,
pinpoints of poison
swelling in the whites.
Little red dots
connecting
one bad decision
to another.
life
in the context
of death approaching,
fears swelling like the
bellies of gods
sickening with
bad-blood-rain
set to spill like anvils
into oceans...
oh the detritus of creation
war and death shaping
nation after nation...
and the pulse
begins to quicken
like the eyes
begin to flutter.
spirits up
and opening backward,
in the dead lake of seeing,
where the whores
change their clothes,
and the deep
hides the meat.
hopes too heavy to float,

drained of life
like the blood of virgins
raised in sacrifice
to the self-made lords,
born of images,
crafted on graves.
mystical truths whored out
to lies we told ourselves
were true.
eyes on the bodies
floating on the blood pools
of dreams,
spinning and twisting
in the sheets of becoming,
becoming fluid,
becoming ruin,
like fruit rotting,
falling blackened and
stinking from the trees.
wilting backward
and pushing
the new death to the
old dying,
living and being
awkward,
resistant,
failed
and damaged.
drowning in rivers
of need,
hungry, greedy
and
spreading
disease.

Spectrum

Listen, listen ...
I forgot to tell you
about the door.
it's not a big deal
but you have to be
careful
not to misjudge.
you know ...
the breadth of the...
just... the uh...
the kind of scope...
or spectrum
that's involved ...
I want to be
real clear...
about that...
I'm so muddy
about so much other shit...
I just want to
be clear about
that one thing.
The thing about
the door is:
it's not a door,
see....it's...
it's a
window.
and that's
an entirely
different
thing.
So listen,

if you're dead set
on going,
just....
stay away
from the
windows,
because they
aren't windows,
the doors are the
windows....and
well....the windows
are the floors.
so remember that,
and also....
don't look in the mirror
but if you do...
don't
let it
see your
eyes.

one too many

I'm sinking,
heavy as the moon
...crawling
toward the sky.
I didn't know
my leg
would cramp up
this morning.
I didn't know
I'd wake up
screaming.
I never
would have guessed
that you could sleep
through all of it.
I know it's a river
and I know it gets
rough.....
but that's not
what's drowning me.
that's not what fails
when I can't
seem to breathe.
it's the turning
and turning,
and the crashing
against the rocks..
so much water
thrashing,
racing toward
the end.
I feel

like that sometimes.
because I dream
like that sometimes.
I know the devils
are feeding
on all my fear,
but they're hungry
and I'm afraid.
with my eyes leaning
toward the back
of the light,
I dreamt
my eyes could fly
but my arms
were weights.
and I fell
to the road and
there were bodies
piled
in front of a gate.
but I did not want
to cross it,
because my head
was just too heavy.
now knowing why
my musing
leads to mourning,
another breakthrough
squandered by
another
one
too many.

never closer

a tender quiet
sucked into
a simple void.
more questions answered
than I care
to remember.
a vast suspicion,
pitted against
a narrow absolution.
my Christian aunts
praying for me.
they shouldn't bother.
suicide
hangs in the air
like four black pills
in a jar.
looking at the mantle,
covered
in dust.
pictures
of dead relatives
and forgotten curios.
we don't discuss it,
what's there to say?
we sit
in separate rooms,
staring blindly
into the
flickering light
of our
personal televisions.
separated

as if by
oceans
or centuries.
separated,
but never
closer together.

Research

two fires in less
than
two hours.
the fire station
is just up the street.
the sirens come through
the windows
like screaming weasels.
someone's trying
to burn down
the neighborhood.
I've been reading books
about serial killers.
I'm interested
in what happens
to people....
what makes them
become monsters.
seems that arson
is often
a prequel
to murder.
I thought about that
as I watched
the curls of
black smoke from my
kitchen window.
thinking: first ash...
then blood,
all this time..
I've had it
backward.

another blackout

quiet now,
a deliberate
side step.
silencing
the screams
of another
aching night.
all for love.
the lines:
crossed,
then forgotten.
leaning heavily
on the
soft
opiate
of denial.
it was not me,
it could not be,
never I,
this way seduced,
never I,
that common,
never I,
so reduced.
red eyes skewed
upon the dawn
of sudden memory.
a blind blinking
toward
a final light....
shining.
another self

dying
cornered
and defiant.
and all at once
the silence,
echoing,
and beckoning,
will toward
change.

Hereditary

My notion of time
is unraveling.
I keep catching
glimpses of something
moving,
just outside my periphery.
I think it's alive.
my face
has been shifting
in the mirror,
trying to
point something out
to me,
but I never get it.
everyday
there's less and less
to hold on to...,
fewer and fewer
absolutes.
when I walk, it's as if I'm
losing my footing,
caught in some gradual,
perpetual fall.
strangers in the street appear
more and more familiar.
I wonder about
parallel existence.
I wonder if something
is about to spill over...
I get the impression
of many,
slowly emerging

selves.
I wake with
a sense of urgency,
and I hurry through my days
trying, in vain
to slow myself down.
my vision is beginning to blur.
I can't help but feel
I've read about this
in books,
but I just
can't remember
and mental
illness
runs
in my
family.

more than you

my kid down there
walking around
under the same sun
you had over you,
and my kid down there...
like I was
your kid
down there,
when he looks up at me,
I remember what I
used to look for
when you were up there,
and I want him
to find it.
cause I didn't
at least not then,
not when you
were up there..
cause you had
nothing for me.
you had nothing.
I got something though
I got something
for my kid down there...
you had it too,
but no balls
to give it
to anyone but
your
self.

my eyes will stop

unwilling to face
the mirror.
not again, never again.
all my sub-selves emerging,
all their faces shifting
and turning
and super imposing.
almost understanding.
terrified
because
once you know something,
it can never be
unknown;
like incest or
cannibalism.
like teeth that
never stop tearing
into flesh,
my eyes never stop
searching
for the center.
I have four other reasons,
for not wanting to eat
the magic mushrooms
anymore. knowing now,
that it's a
kind of death.
I tend to
steer clear and
avoid the subject
whenever it arises.
the Yaqui way

of knowledge and
the second ring
of power.
sometimes
I remember dreams
and imagine
that my waking fade
of all the details are my
dream-self forgetting
that my real life was
just a dream.
I know
any day now
I'll stop walking,
forever,
I'll stop seeing
forever..
I won't believe
in anything
I won't fear death.
my heart
will stop beating
and everything
I have ever
been
will cease.
the knowledge
brings
no comfort.
it doesn't
bring anything
at all.

mass-of-man

oh what have we done?
our platform headed children
petitioning poisons,
training their minds,
like dogs,
to speak of their chains
in tongues.
to bay up at the
tower of epiphanies
that looms
bliss less and
unreachable
like the memory
of all our courage.
this sad mass of man
we've made:
convinced and complacent,
cornered and mistaken,
with our enlightened
darkened,
our prophets
shrunken
and freedom,
finally:
sectioned, sanctioned,
and packaged
in plastic.
oh with our reverence reduced
to idle consumer
contemplation,
and this ever present
air of contentment,

fouling us like
some rotted meat
stuck between teeth
as the puppets,
lead we,
their strings,
astray.
blind and baffled
from funeral to parade,
just as dead as we
deserve.
this is our time,
we believe
victorious at last,
blind as the past.
dead as we ever wanted,
as the cancers
hand out pamphlets,
to the Christians
about the rapture.
feeding and feeding
on our need to believe,
what the grand inquisitor
dared to question.
the audacity of our surprise
to see so much greed
in our own eyes...
the irony of our ambition
converting to entitlement.
no wonder our inheritance
bought us nothing but
an ancestry of blood.
what did we expect
having invested nothing?

Butcher Hail!

Oh pentacle of lost transit.
Harbinger of death's loose chains.
Oh deep mother of dying swarms,
lend chaos its hiss and chatter,
that the brethren may rise
to the pulpits of neon flicker.
Hail to the dying eyes!
Hail to the prophet margins!
Arise our sleeping soldiers of ruin,
the war machine has idled too long.
The gears in need of blood and bone.
This famine has caught the scent
of our defeat,
the stink of our fear.
Let blind hatred reign,
let greed pull our masses
into tattered braids of fury.
Murder sings that our
inheritance be complete.
That our tongues fork in the
fashion of our ancestry,
of our superiority.
Hail the butcher!
Hail the worm!
The maggot!
The swarm of us...
the hive of us....
HAIL!
HAIL!

making peace

a scarred moon,
nippled and pockmarked
by all our musing.
the night offering
nothing but trouble.
I sit quietly
on my easy chair,
but nothing is easy.
draining one beer
after the next,
in a dizzied state of
mourning
and compressing,
years of traumas,
into flashes of pain.
my genitals swollen
and stinging with desire.
with nothing
on the horizon
but more and more
waiting....
more and more
wanting.
yet I don't resent
my all too
human condition,
keenly aware
of what
I signed up for,
and how
or when
I could expect it

to deliver.
making peace
with the warlords
of all my
restless
selves.
resigning them
to silence.

Carpe Diem

just remember,
the day is
what you make it.
the spirit,
is how.
and,
as with anything,
love it,
regardless.

mission

It was my dad's
party.
all his friends
were there.
I was twelve.
I kept sneaking drinks
from the adults.
every time they
got up to dance
I took hits from every
drink at the table,
then my dad
threw me
in the shower
because he said
I was humiliating
the both of us.
I dashed out
in my underwear
soaking wet
and tried to
dance with all the girls
at once.
my dad carried me
into the bedroom,
draping my drunk body
over his shoulder,
throwing me onto the bed.
down deep
I think
I wanted
to kill him

but
humiliation
would have
to do.
the next morning
I woke to find
I had vomited
all over myself
and had also
shit my pants.
my dad walked in
and looked down at me
in shame
and disgust.
mission:
accomplished.

Where I can be Found

In the dead pan eyes
of the damned,
buying blood milk
for the babies.
in line waiting
to be punished,
all fevers and
death rattles,
in league with
ghosts dragging
their feet in the dark.
in the arms of loves
lost and sacrificed
under four dead moons
that shine and shine.
in the hearts of dolls with
little rubies for eyes,
flashing back from
one dark mirror
after another.
in the sick air
of reason turning tricks
to pay over and over
for the same mistakes.
In the crippled veins
of the ever slowing heartbeat,
in the belly of the beast,
in the heart of the sun.

V

Untitled paranoia rant #81

The fear comes and I coil myself into a corner
where the insects hiss bad dreams into my
open ears and the blood pools in the pockets
of memories where all those broken lives
try over and over to mend themselves but can't
and it's not me dying in here anymore, it's we
and we can't live like this anymore because
of them and what their god damn meanings
keep pushing me toward believing and I won't
not because I can't but because I know I shouldn't
and all my hiding becomes this smell I can't get rid
of tentacles of thinking sucking at me from behind
my fluttering eyes that won't stop blinking or
weeping or feigning sleep that won't come waiting
for something soft and calm to wash over me and
keep me still and safe from
the rabid dogs that can smell the smell I can't
get rid of cause it's me and my disease that won't heal
the fear that won't let go... and I crawl beneath the
sheets or under the bed...
or I hide in the closet or drive and drive in the dark,
avoiding my mirrors
because my eyes are in there where I can see them
and I don't want to see them because I know where
they've been and the worse thing is knowing if I were
blind, the dark would be even worse.

Portals (or finding god after 72 hours, up on speed)

I can feel us shaking.
It's been another one of those nights.
The fabric between the worlds
seems to have thinned,
almost to the point of breaking.
I can see things moving on
the other side,
silhouettes, dancing
in terrible circles.
and I can't remember
which one of us led
the other here this time.
memories seem to be
fusing and melding
into one
vast
experience,
timeless and recurring.
the air breathes in
and out of the sky.
there is a vague
sense of shadow.
It's as if we wait
for the grand explanation
to materialize.
some symbol
that will weave
all the little
chaotic tendrils
of nervous thinking
into one unified
coil of purpose.

our desperate waiting
mirroring
the exaltation of prayer.
but there is no explanation.
only questions mounting
and stacking
upon themselves;
mystical parodies of
sacred geometry.
the dark architecture
of anti-reason,
spawning structures
of transcendence.
wedged into the earth
like ancient markers
of confirmation.
awaiting the proper
speculation
to unravel its secrets
and make naked
its truth.
lost in tombs
the shape of portals.
and we shake
at the brink
of understanding,
prolonging the epiphany
for as long as we dare.
clinging to our ignorance
like frightened children
peering
into
the vastness of discovery.
I can feel us shaking.

congregating
at the precipice.
believing.
hoping that
what has led us here
will become tangible enough
to love.
but there is only us,
as we turn
toward each other,
finally understanding:
it is love,
our love,
and
nothing
else.
knowing this
will be
as close
to god
as we will
ever
get.

Con-Verted

My ex-girlfriend
had a brother
in prison
for bank robbery.
she had pictures of him
holding a rifle
in one hand,
a bag of money
in the other.
he was a white boy
but when we went
down to the federal
holding facility,
to slip him ten sticky
balloons of heroin,
he appeared
conspicuously Mexican.
he wore his hair
all slicked back,
had a fat moustache,
and tattoos of
naked Mexican women
with beautifully round breasts.
he spoke with an accent
that sounded like
every single one of my
dead uncle's homeboys.
he mixed English with
bits of broken Spanish
it was strange.
my ex asked him about it,
he said the peckerwoods

were outnumbered,
besides which,
they were stupid.
he said that nobody
protected their own people
like the *raza* did.
I noticed a tattoo on his neck
that read *Huero*.
in old English lettering..
he was a cool motherfucker,
all her other brothers
turned out to be
racist
redneck
speed freak
alcoholics,
but this one,
this one
was alright.

Beats?

Fuck the BEATS!
I don't want to hear
about the fucking BEATS!
The beats sucked on
each other's dicks,
drank wine,
shitted and vomited,
took small chances.
the beats fucked
each others wives
then fucked each
other!
the beats never
chiseled through
anything
with their fingers,
they had soft hands!
I have soft hands!
fuck me too,
fuck poetry,
I don't want to talk
about fucking *poetry!*

ruin

hurting for quiet
but wanting noise
more than ever.
lost between
escaping
and succumbing,
drinking in order
to revert
back to where
it was
I turned
that corner.
soon
I'm too drunk
to remember
if I was
even driving.
I've been
pushing harder
on the pedals.
looking harder
seeing harder
hard up
all the time.
so many legs
and hips and
eyes and hair.
a carnival of noise
in my eyes
and loins
and all I want
is to shut it

all
down.
please,
before
I ruin
everything.

Good Times (for Kim)

Tell me about that time you flipped out on acid because you thought it was the end of the world and the cats were turning into giant rats in the street and the walls were melting and some spray paint on the walls that looked like blood and you thought the building was dying and you were crying and so wishing you had just done some coke instead. tell me about the time you did too much coke and everywhere you turned someone was offering you some for free and you couldn't turn it down cause it was so free and tempting but then people's faces started doing funny things and you called me from a pay phone half crying but too high to cry really and you said all the people were demons and you wanted to know how all those people could be demons and you thought I might have some answers because of my experience with demons. I remember you drove to a friend's house for some solace but she was real high on crack and had a whole fucking mountain of it on her living room table and she offered it to you saying you could have as much as you wanted and tell my why you did some anyway even though you were already flipping out and then you called me again and asked me to pick you up cause you were sure you were going to die and didn't want to die alone and there you were in the back seat of the stanza and I played you some tender music and you cried like a baby and when you got to my house you kept squeezing the kids like you wanted to suck the innocence right out of them and it made me kind of uncomfortable because I had seen that vampire side of you before and you swore and swore that you were

off that shit forever and that was like six years ago so
how come we were doing some coke just a few weeks
ago at our house and everything seemed really ok
and fun and now you want to come over and do it
again real soon because you had such a good time
and you were real comfortable and you thought
maybe your trouble with coke was that you weren't
doing it with the right people and maybe you should
just do it with us. don't get me wrong it's not that I
don't want you to come over with a bunch of coke,
because I do and I had fun too it's just that I trip out
on how it's all so fucking random and bullshit and
cyclical it keeps coming back around like it's all
brand new like drinking or fucking or anything....just
these cycles ...I pay attention cause I don't want to
demon up on you and I don't want you to demon up
on me cause I'm afraid if you do I'll have to ask you
to leave and I'll probably convince you to leave the
coke with us, for your own safety you understand,
but I love you and it's really all ok and soon you'll be
really dead like everyone else and then who will give
a fuck how much coke you did right? so call me later
and we'll see what's up, I get paid on Friday.

take the reins

I've been hiding again.
behind ...
things to remember
and
things to do.
It's easy,
when you're busy.
Tougher when
nothing stands between
you
and the dark.
So I...
answer
the phone,
agree to
someone else's plans.
night,
after night,
I find myself,
raising beer cans
to the sky,
toasting death,
life,
and struggle.
a sea
of blank eyes
glittering from my couch.
smiling
and pretending,
they're interested
in what I'm saying,
and me pretending

my mind's not on
the roaches
again.
waiting,
in vain,
for someone else
to take the reins,
and pull us all
somewhere
far from here.
and when
at last
I choose to emerge,
I am always alone
and too far away
to participate.

hope

like a tiny star...
or a child's
little laughter...
so easy to miss....
you could breathe
one good breath
and miss it
and you do....
and you're
so sorry...
you could cry...
and you do...
and it
does nothing
to help you
and it hurts
so much more
than you
would have
imagined ...
and you imagined it
so many times before
that when it
finally happened ...
it was like
a memory ....
and you remembered it
like you always will.....
slow
and close
to your
trembling heart.

Hand Me Down

This stick poking
at the dead body
of small boy me
now only this
bad smell rising
that I cover up with
bad blankets of
mustered up memories.
Anything bad enough
to compete with the
stink of your
resentment.
Like I asked
to shoot out of you.
Like I enjoy being
a consequence of your
stupid sex. Rather I'd be
dead seed splattered
onto stinking gutter,
but no, you had to
slip it to my mother,
knowing she couldn't
take it but you
took her anyway
thinking the ride
would be worth it
and it wasn't and
oh how I
make you remember.
Bad stupid you
shining on face of
stupid me and you

couldn't take it
or give it back.
So you hated cause that
was manly and how manly
you tried and tried to
believe you could be.
And me having seen
more of a man
in a tree, or a flower,
or a puppy, or a girl,
more of a man
I saw
in everything
that was not you.
A man? No no, not you,
not now, not then,
not ever.
The coward that hid
behind the stupid
mask of your distaste.
How you marveled
and rambled
at the boy that
could not be, no not
yours, how could I
have come from you?
And the question hanging
like a dead man
for both of us
Swinging
back and forth,
from me, to you,
and you to me.
And this page

only to be rid of you
once and for all.
So it is
that I return
your inheritance,
unwanted
and
unopened.

moth wing tea

*You should never
kill moths,*
she warned,
recounting
her grandmother's
hand-me-down
myths.

*moths are the vessels
for souls
in transit,
and killing them
will trap them
between
the worlds
forever.*

and I could not
bring myself
to tell her,
that killing them
was just
the beginning,
of what ,
I actually,
had in mind.

meth-scape

arms, like ribs,
pulled over
my heart.
a cacophony of beating
and breathing.
waves and waves
of fear,
rippling over
a glistening skin.
the damp pillow,
smashed beneath
my restless face.
one train of thought
crashing
into the next.
nothing to separate
the dreams from
the memories.
and the old familiar
panic... nestles in,
like a swarm of bees,
humming in my ear.
two white pills,
one yellow
and two blue...
all racing
the second hand
of the clock ticking...
and ticking
night toward dawn.
mumbling prayers
and making promises,

revealing secrets
and confessing sins....
all just lost
to the drone of stars,
silent as sentinels.
no answers,
no revelations,
just a quiet
knowing.
and the gentle
whispers
of voices with nothing
but questions
to pose.
trying to put faces
on the blank
of the void.
restless again.
nervous again.
lost as always.
deciding finally,
that finding,
like believing,
only brings me....
back
to my self
back to where
I was
trying
to escape.

Vision Quest: Manhattan Beach
(psilocybin by the ocean)

It's not easy to
think of yourself
in those terms...
when the dolphins
come up for air,
and throw you
their deep black eyes
and challenge your
notions of matter
and element.
when the sea
becomes something
you breathe,
and the sand shakes like
you could drown in it.
the air becomes heavy
and the people become
as alien as fluorescent light,
and your feelings of ugly
turn in your stomach
like the cramps of too many
visions ingested at once.
some Indian thing
comes to mind as the
shapes and patterns
flow out of a slit
in the sky,
and you think
you remember
something you read,
though thinking in language

has become as silly as
propelling yourself
by moving your legs,
as the dolphins dip and circle
and come up for drinks
of the heavy air,
sucking it back like smoke,
glancing over
to make sure you're looking.
and the birds
like drunken fish,
in the pool of the clouds,
looking down for the
right pair of eyes
to shit on and they're
mine and they're mine.
and you look
for any signs
of love or hope,
or meaning,
but it all melts away
in a wave of terror that
hits you in the center
of your turning stomach,
cause it's too much
to know that you've
had it all wrong
all along
and all of it's
a lie and you don't
know if this might
be a peek into your
next level perception.
but this is not the kind of thing

you thought you would be
on the other side
of it all,
cause all that you'd heard
led you to believe...

never mind
I've said too much already.
it was nothing.
it was just the beach.
nothing happened.
I was high I guess.
I shouldn't get
so high.
I was tripping
never mind...
it was all
in my mind.

desperate like that

I miss driving too fast
when it was too late
at night.
flying down the 110
to the 5
to state park.
I miss
whistling drunk
into the dark.
seeing the eyes
slipping out of
the shadows.
the exchange of money
for wack.
all the slang,
and haggling,
and determining
just
how strong
the shit actually was.
I miss
the triumphant ride
back to the pad.
down the 5
to the 110
to the street
with the tree.
I miss
not being able
to wait.
hitting that shit
in the car,

on the freeway,
driving with my
knee.
I miss it because
I'm just not
that desperate
anymore.
not about that.
not about anything.
I want to be
desperate like that
again.
I want to be
more
like that
again.
because I feel
so safe now.
no danger
anywhere.
and it
just
doesn't
feel
right.

left to be

damp mud fist
of big ton tone.
blood bone hammer
pounding down
over dead bodies.
minutes killing hours,
linear lanced eternal.
broken circles succumbing
to tired lines.
astronomers curling up
in their graves.........
eye holes spilling over
with the dust of
so much seen,
and the blur of years,
just leaves falling
dead from trees.
meat at war
with matter,
Einstein
batting eyelashes
at Jesus.
rains of people
thinking louder and louder,
a cacophony of wailing,
up to the
piss yellow moon.
waves of chemicals
crashing silently
in our brains
that we ingest to
sedate and abate,

all to no avail
as the lids
flutter over
our upturned eyes.
with nothing left
to see,
and no one
left
to *be*.

counting

as the moon shook
snakes from her
hair,
raining,
writhing
tangled dreams,
I slept
and dreamt
of your
spreading legs.
and when
the sun
finally burned
the dark
from my eyes,
I opened them
to find that
you had gone.
and I closed them
wondering how long
before
I would
never have to
open them
again.

clear

carousels of bending limbs,
flickers of the blood light
shining....on
bouncing bones erected
into fences and walls.
torsos bruised by
capillaries singing
death's hymn:
an ode to disease.
escape hindered,
mired in desire.
butchers lined up in
meat's procession,
oh that the blood might cleanse
our filthy genitals
swelling and volleying
for position.
church bells ringing
in the halls of surrender,
the soft insanity of faith,
seductive and forgiving;
ape spit shining
in the orifice of dreams.
funerals of joy
bedding down heavy
with eyes turned back
to the excess of abandon,
because the dark there
pleasures
deep as the menstrual ruins.
our cavernous nature calling,
pearls of semen pulsing

beneath flesh
taxed and stretched.
the occupation of deliverance.
irrational fears entwined into
the braided ropes of our denial.
limp bodies piled one atop the other.
maggot blankets of
slithering suffocation.
wet beds of shame and
the arbitrary betrayal of instinct.
mind against compulsion.
fever forcing fire into submission.
the reeling thoughts
left to their own devices
and the absolute
coffins of finality,
smug and convinced,
buried and inarguable.
the death of being,
contorting
the trembling limbs
of reaching and reaching...
eyes into wells, souls into hells...
fumbling and groping in the dark
tiring and slipping downward
in the dark...
seeing... finally seeing...
clearly in the dark.

Brazen Enough

I'll stand for
nothing less than
your scalpel fingers
on my bloated flesh.
send your butchers,
your saviors,
your innocent
dreams...my need
to feed
is brutal
and primal.
oh my cannibal tongue,
flicking
in and out of
your artifice.
these nightmares
speak volumes,
utter graves.
let's slip down
into the bosom
of our dead
mothers...
let's slip down
into our
lost forgottens.
that we may
one day
rise,
from the ashes
of our
fusion.
no god left

to save
or absolve.
no Satan
brazen enough
to challenge,
or threaten,
our blissed out
eyes.
because now
we see
what was not
there.
because now
we believe
what we would not
dare:
that all of us
is we,
burning
in a hell
of need

Boredom

sat there
looking toward
the television,
but not actually
watching it.
It was a hot day
and I was
tired.
I waited
for something
to do.
I waited
for something
to occur to me.
I got up, urinated,
sat back down,
continued
waiting.
It was like
dying.
I thought:
this must be what
cancer patients
do.
Then I thought
well,
if I had cancer,
this is what
I'd do.
I got up
ate some cheese,
sat back down.

slept a bit,
my head
rolling around.
dreaming,
remembering how
my mother
killed herself,
waking
baffled
suddenly wondering
was it boredom?
is that why
she did it?
and if it was,
how bored
do you have
to get?

comforted (for Thelma)

dead end job
free of aspiration,
free of ambition.
a lonely hope
pulled up
like a blanket
against a cold
and unforgiving
routine.
blind to the
motions that
keep the wolves
at bay.
a pleasant dark
unfolding
like a cool,
clean fog,
rolling in
with all the
promise
of a well
kept
secret.
nine to five
then seven
to twelve.
the numbers,
more relevant
than the moments
they confine.
and I sleep,
comforted by the

easy lies I lay
my head upon.
it's no wonder
the days
infringe
upon the nights.
all I've
sacrificed
to the lull
of flickering lights,
and pulsing loins.
I welcome
my well-earned
death.
ready to die now,
my time has
come,
ready to be
happy,
now
that this
living's
done.

back into your hole

you're a bad monkey
and no one did this zoo to you
but yourself.
it's been weeks and weeks
of nothing but,
dead skin flakes and looking
in the stainless steel plate
that was left
to serve
as a blurry mirror.
what did you expect,
to find in there?
you can smell
the urine mixing
with the blood
can't you?
is it effective?
is it the odor
that drives you
back into your hole?
you look good
looking out, from your
hole.
you look good hiding
in there,
full of terror and
unanswered questions.
don't worry
eventually you'll die
perhaps then
you'll get to
crawl out

into something new
perhaps then
you can be
more than you are
now.

as bad as it is

parades of people
walking
limping.
a bad time to be
lost in the city.
there is a fever out there
coming to get us.
arsenals of daring
and luring and
summoning.
we die
when living
is done,
but not before...
and if it
seems unfair,
it's only because
we're blind
with lasting.
a hungry fame
pulling our hearts
from our eyes.
with all this fire
burning..
it's no wonder
we sweat
in our dreams.
waking at two and three
and four in the morning.
to turn on the fan,
to turn off the fan.
it's my period,

it's my jones
it's my bad day at work ....
it's my numbers,
it's my bones.
yeah I know
we're all going to die,
some laughing,
some screaming,
some fading,
some gleaming.
and knowing
never helps, never stops
the dogs from barking
or the truth
from failing.
parades and ceremonies...
lost in love
in lust,
in losing. coughing
and coughing
and coughing
and coughing.
another day knowing
we've made it
as bad
as it is.

shooting in los angeles

crouching down
with my camera,
trying to get
as beneath
as I can.
I shoot churches
and legs
this way.
because I want
the sense
of being overwhelmed.
all that symbolism,
and power looming
over me,
like the moonlight
shining over
a dead lake.
I want to masturbate
to the churches,
and pray
to the legs,
but I
can't get
either going
for too long
before
I get distracted.
So I crouch down
with my camera
and shoot
something
else.

anniversary

making dolls
in the dark,
a stitch of skin...
for the dresses,
blood
for color.
fear for the eyes
and longing
for the hands.
up late again,
making dolls.
dolls to
lay on your grave,
because
your anniversary
approaches,
and I want
to commemorate
with more
than dead flowers,
and fading memories.
I want to resurrect
the connection
of mother
and son.
giver
and taker.
making dolls
in the dark,
away
from the light.

adversary poem #67

and your eyes
became mouths
and the teeth
of all your starving,
reeked with meat
stuck in-between.
all your murders,
stinking of the killing
of all your seeing.
and your tongue
became tentacle
that forked and
sucked
and writhed,
in languages that swirled
like razor blades,
and you were puzzled
because I was not afraid,
surprised because
I could reply
and relate.
and the shift
in the shape
of your terrible face,
did nothing to change
the love for your hate.
so we danced
and you thought
we were fighting,
and you smiled
while I fucked you,
thinking you'd won.

witnessed

A cat carcass
on the freeway,
its entrails spilling
out onto the asphalt

A young boy
stabbed to death
in the parking lot
of a popular
fast food restaurant.
his blood spilling
out of his back

A run over pigeon
fluttering its
broken wings
in the street
speckles of blood
spewing from its beak.

A half dead rat
dangling from a
giant mousetrap
two inches
over my head
back broken
screaming.

Approximately
seven human heads
in plastic
zip lock bags

in the freezer of
a friend
one of which
I held
in my hands

my dead mother's face
mouth open,
scream frozen,
covered in vomit
and charcoal

my father,
laughing
at me.

looking forward

what will be left of us
when our chests
rise and fall
for the last time?
what will we see
when our eyes
turn to dust?
and what of
our desire?
will it rest
like the meat
on our bones
will fall?
and what
is to come
of our faith?
perhaps
new questions
will arise...
perhaps...not.
only one thing
is certain.
I will
never have to
endure
another one
of our
inane conversations.
something
to look
forward to
I guess.

forever

Today:
a trumpet
for your eyes,
all the stars
in the sky,
burning
to light the way...
to maneuver
through the dark
of so much nothing.
I hope
there's something
out there,
but I hope it's not
the same for me
as it is,
for you.
I hope that *what*
and *how*
we do it,
shapes
where
and how,
we get there.
it's not that
I never want to
see you again,
I just hope
that neither of us
will look
the same.
I hope that

all we did
when we
could have
done nothing,
will leave us
shining,
and forever
changed.

The End

Dennis Cruz is a Los Angeles native who has been writing prose, poetry and fiction for over 20 years. Born in San Jose, Costa Rica, his family immigrated to the U.S. when he was just an infant. His work has been featured on public radio stations KPFK and KXLU, and he has performed extensively throughout the Los Angeles area. He has featured his work in many Los Angeles literary establishments, including: Beyond Baroque, Skylight Books and The World Stage. He was also selected as one of the newer poets to watch by the ALOUD series at the Los Angeles Public Library. He lives in North-East Los Angeles with his wife and son.

More about the Book and the Author

"Dennis Cruz makes us laugh to keep from crying. Like a narrator for the destitute, he weaves his dark poetic tales with a sly humor that comforts those who have been there."
- Joe Baiza, guitarist, *Saccharine Trust*

"Part Charles Bukowski, part Hunter S. Thompson and all Dennis Cruz, this Los Angeles wordslinger is the real deal, terrifying and terrifyingly beautiful. Honest and human to a fault, meat to the bone. Nasty, raw, streetwise, smart, laugh out loud funny, outrageous, iconoclastic and one of the best damn poets writing in America right now. Sip Cruz's Moth Wing Tea, a strong dose of something sacred that is guaranteed to take you higher or you can come find me and kick my old grey ass."
- S.A. Griffin, Editor of *The Outlaw Bible of American Poetry*

"Dennis Cruz writes the poetry of dark and lovely gods that live in the every day, and I mean every day: DMV toilet, telephone poles on the street on the way home, living room looking at wall and wife. Moth Wing Tea is not just a beautiful book, it's the real Los Angeles literature. I'm so happy that it is out and I can carry it with me. Yes, the planet is more alive now!"
- Steve Abee, author of *Johnny Future*

"Dennis Cruz's poems will make you feel simultaneously uncomfortable, vulnerable, unholy, and powerless. His work is unafraid of intermingling emotions of humor and sensuality, as it navigates through the landscape of Los Angeles, while providing a voice and humanity to addiction and rehabilitation."
- Luivette Resto, author of *Unfinished Portrait* and *Ascension*

"How do we translate the unspeakable language of grief? In the short, harrowing lines of MOTH WING TEA, Dennis Cruz gives us his answer. This is the poetics of survival: no adornment, no romanticizing; only the simple, methodical imagery of a poet saying out loud. The juxtaposition of fresh paint, chrome, and a suffering body. The world as explained by one who knows there is more to this life than simply getting up for work. The unvarnished descriptions of violence. The voice of Dennis Cruz weaves together a patchwork of tragedies into a manifesto for poets in the 21st century. As the poet says: "the fear was never/meant/to dissuade you,/but only/to heighten/your senses." Read this book, and get to work."

-Rich Villar, Executive Director, Acentos

Other Punk Hostage Press Titles

'Fractured' (2012) by Danny Baker

'Better Than A gun In A knife Fight' (2012) by A. Razor

'The Daughters of Bastards' (2012) by Iris Berry

'Drawn Blood: Collected Works from D.B.P.Ltd., 1985--1995' (2012) by A. Razor

'impress' (2012) by C.V. Auchterlonie

'Tomorrow, Yvonne- Poetry & Prose for Suicidal Egoists' (2012) by Yvonne De la Vega

'Beaten Up Beaten Down' (2012) by A. Razor

'miracles of the BloG: A series' (2012) by Carolyn Srygley--Moore

'8th & Agony' (2012) by Rich Ferguson

'Untamed' (2013) by Jack Grisham